To look for other titles in this series, visit www.tcpress.com

continued

Early Childhood Education Series, *continued*

Transforming Early Years Policy in the U.S.

A Call to Action

Edited by Mark K. Nagasawa, Lacey Peters,
Marianne N. Bloch, and Beth Blue Swadener

Foreword by Mariana Souto-Manning

TEACHERS COLLEGE PRESS

TEACHERS COLLEGE | COLUMBIA UNIVERSITY
NEW YORK AND LONDON

Published by Teachers College Press,® 1234 Amsterdam Avenue, New York, NY 10027

Front cover graphics by Hey Rabbit / The Noun Project.
Figure 17.2 used with permission of Freya Bloomberg.

Library of Congress Cataloging-in-Publication Data
Names: Nagasawa, Mark K., editor. | Peters, Lacey, editor. | Bloch, Marianne N., editor. | Swadener, Beth Blue, editor.
Title: Transforming early years policy in the U.S. : a call to action / edited by Mark K. Nagasawa, Lacey Peters, Marianne N. Bloch, and Beth Blue Swadener ; foreword by Mariana Souto-Manning.
Description: New York, NY : Teachers College Press, 2023. | Series: Early childhood education series | Includes bibliographical references and index. | Summary: "This accessible collection examines some of the most urgent policy issues facing early childhood care and education in the United States. Centering the perspectives of Black, Indigenous, and other People of Color, chapters advance practice-based recommendations for how the nation's inequitable systems can be transformed"—Provided by publisher.
Identifiers: LCCN 2022038183 (print) | LCCN 2022038184 (ebook) | ISBN 9780807768143 (paperback) | ISBN 9780807768150 (hardback) | ISBN 9780807781623 (ebook)
Subjects: LCSH: Early childhood education—United States. | Minorities—Education (Early childhood)—United States. | Early childhood teachers—United States. | Educational change—United States.
Classification: LCC LB1139.25 .T698 2023 (print) | LCC LB1139.25 (ebook) | DDC 372.210973—dc23/eng/20220922
LC record available at https://lccn.loc.gov/2022038183
LC ebook record available at https://lccn.loc.gov/2022038184

ISBN 978-0-8077-6814-3 (paper)
ISBN 978-0-8077-6815-0 (hardcover)
ISBN 978-0-8077-8162-3 (ebook)

Printed on acid-free paper
Manufactured in the United States of America

Contents

Foreword

(De)Liberating Early Years Policy: Toward Full and True Belonging

Mariana Souto-Manning, Erikson Institute

Historical analysis shows that while policies often purport to improve early years education, many have upheld inequities (Part I of this volume). Intersectional systems of inequity that present in early years contexts affect the everyday lives of teachers, caregivers, and young children—especially those who are Black, have dis/abilities, and are identifiable along other axes of oppression (Collins, 2019; see Chapter 17 of this volume for more detail)—yet deep considerations of (in)equities are not often reflected in early years policies. Furthermore, when early years educator-practitioners and researchers think of policymakers, they rarely see themselves represented. Delineations of policymaking tend to omit important voices, experiences, and wisdom from the field in favor of longstanding societal power hierarchies that tend to uphold borders and maintain consistent boundaries between those who decide and those who are decided about (Yuval-Davis et al., 2019).

This edited collection seeks to advance critical early years policy (de)liberations toward belonging, highlighting how "processes of belonging/ not belonging are rarely articulated, except when belonging is under threat" (Sumsion & Wong, 2011, p. 33) and troubling externally imposed categories that (de)limit belonging. Who is assumed to belong in early years policymaking? Who is immediately attributed belonging? Related explorations unpack a process in which early years educators and researchers, as well as family and community members, are situated as outsiders to early years policy, reflecting ongoing power dynamics in society that have direct inclusion and exclusion implications. This pattern is visible in the de/professionalization of early years professionals (Part IV) and the subjugation and marginalization of their experiences, perspectives, voices, and values in early years policymaking and policy outcomes.

Seeking to (de)liberate early years policy, chapters in this edited collection take up questions such as: Who decides who belongs? On what grounds are judgments of inclusion and exclusion made? How are borders delineated and how permeable are they? Can early years practitioners (also) become early years policymakers? Both individual and collective positionings are fluid, contestable, and changeful, yet those with power mobilize resources and deploy tactics to maintain their privilege and positioning in (and through) early years policy. Resistance, on the other hand, takes shape as teachers strategically and deliberately engage in policystretching and policybreaking, supported by communities (Part V) and via policies and practices that center anti-racism in early years contexts (Part II).

In this book, border-crossing possibilities come to life, inviting us to reconfigure familiar boundaries and foment resistance to established policies and policymakers. Importantly, though, to belong should not—does not—mean to assimilate. hooks (2015) poignantly explained that assimilation is "a strategy deeply rooted in the ideology of white supremacy and its advocates urge black people to negate blackness, to imitate racist white people so as to better absorb their values, their way of life" (p. 113). As you read these chapters and reflect on how early years professionals engage in the (de)liberation work of imagining and attaining belonging in and through early years policy, of seeing themselves and other agentively *without* containment or assimilation, please consider the detrimental consequences such approaches seek to avoid.

Early years professionals have long been pressured to perform belonging and pretend to understand the processes, actors, and rationale of early years policy that entails harmful practices associated with assimilation. Conventional norms of assimilation pressure individuals to engage in self-inscriptions, crafting new identity stories, mobilizing resources, and deploying other tactics to tell themselves and others who they need to be and not be to belong, borders that exclude and subjugate. This book takes an oppositional approach, offering a rich and textured mosaic of counterstories to the assimilative pressures of bidding for and performing belonging in early years policy (Souto-Manning & Rabadi-Raol, 2018). (De)liberating early years policy means deliberately refusing to see early years practice and policy as separate from policymaking. It means (re)positioning early years practitioners and researchers as policymakers, with the recognition that there is more expertise across early years practitioners, researchers, and policymakers than in any one group. It entails expanding relations, learning from communities of color, and cultivating the ongoing engagement of communities (Part VII). It requires exploring the fluidity of borders that include and exclude, abolishing them deliberately toward freedom and liberation. This is a call to collective action—toward a future for early years education that does not yet exist; a future wherein policies consistently abandon the prioritized notion of expectability to instead embrace and nurture potentialities.

REFERENCES

Collins, P. H. (2019). *Intersectionality as critical social theory*. Duke University Press.

hooks, b. (2015). *Talking back: thinking feminist, thinking Black*. Routledge.

Souto-Manning, M., & Rabadi-Raol, A. (2018). (Re)Centering quality in early childhood education: Toward intersectional justice for minoritized children. *Review of Research in Education*, *42*(1), 203–225.

Sumsion, J., & Wong, S. (2011). Interrogating 'belonging' in belonging, being and becoming: The early years learning framework for Australia. *Contemporary Issues in Early Childhood*, *12*(1), 28–45.

Yuval-Davis, N., Wemyss, G., & Cassidy, K. (2019). *Bordering*. John Wiley & Sons.

Acknowledgments

We imagined this book as both a provocation and illustration of ways in which early years policies and practices are being reimagined by educators every day. The result far exceeds our imaginations. This is because the many contributors to this volume generously gave their expertise and devoted considerable time to be in dialogue with us and one another. In these days of pandemic and political rancor, when early childhood care and education's essentialness was both clarified and dismissed in national discourse, we found hope in one another's stories and commitments. Within the editorial team, our intergenerational and reciprocal learning was a joy.

We appreciate Sarah Biondello and the trust she had in this project from the outset. We wish her well as she transitions into retirement. We give thanks to the reviewers of the proposal who offered valuable feedback as we conceptualized how this book would take shape. And now we are very grateful to Sarah Jubar for taking up the torch and guiding us through the last phases of this volume's publication and for the supportive production team at Teachers College Press, led by managing editor Mike Olivo and marketing manager Nancy Power.

Finally, we dedicate this book to the early years practitioners who have long labored in challenging conditions, while holding strong to a vision of well-being for young children that foregrounds equity, inclusion, belonging, and the possibility of transformation for our field and society.

Transforming Early Years Policy in the U.S.

Introduction

Mark K. Nagasawa, Lacey Peters, Marianne N. Bloch, and Beth Blue Swadener

This is a very different kind of early years policy book. First, we use the term *early years*, reflecting what early childhood is called in many other nations. This is both a subtle way of calling attention to the need for us to think differently about early childhood care and education (ECE), and recognition that there are lessons to be learned from how other nations approach early years policy, although this collection's focus is on the United States.

Second, this book is guided by the belief that much of the academic literature addressing early years policies is overly jargony and omits voices, experiences, and wisdom from the field. This separates educators, researchers, and advocates, which undermines our shared goal of creating an equitable society. Therefore, when we say *policies,* we are referring to rules that tell people what to do. This can include formal policies like laws, regulations, and court rulings, but it also encompasses organizational policies, less formal *guidance* from a regulatory body like a department of education or board of directors, and even *unwritten rules* that folx follow.

This book is also different in that it is dialogic by design. We invited a group of expert educator-advocates, educator-scholars, and scholar-advocates to share their experiences and critiques of major early years policies in the United States. This is not criticism for criticism's sake, as is too often the case. Rather, our colleagues offer experience-based recommendations that can be acted upon. Not easily, quickly, or without debate, but acted upon nonetheless.

In the spirit of "convivial research and insurgent learning" (Callahan, 2018), we engaged our colleagues in ongoing conversations, individually and through both small- and large-group meetings. (If there can be a positive by-product of the COVID-19 pandemic, it has been to show how technology can be used to form relationships, break down silos, and bridge distances.) We then asked our colleagues to write short essays analyzing enduring issues in the field—always through equity lenses. Throughout the book, we distinguish between equity and equality. This is important because ideas about equality are often expressed by trying to treat everyone the same. Equity praxis (theory into practice) means confronting inequitable histories and social conditions, and providing the necessary, differentiated resources to pay reparations for these.

The majority read one another's pieces. This led to lively discussions and at times debates over policy options and priorities. While there was debate, you will also see considerable agreement. This book is a provocation of hope, extending across time and space, intended to stimulate further dialogue, encourage imagining possibilities where none seem evident, and catalyze collective action.

BACKGROUND AND CONTEXT

The idea for this project began just before the 2020 presidential election, while discussing what we would want a new administration to do. It turned out that the Biden administration had ideas—somewhat surprising ones, including $400 billion in federal funding for universal preschool for 3- and 4-year-olds and affordable child care (Koch, 2021). That kind of money could make a meaningful difference for folx.

However, we were also concerned about *how* that funding would be used, *where* it would go, and *who* would be making decisions about these things. Our concerns echoed ones shared by W. Steven Barnett, Director of the National Institute for Early Education Research, nearly 30 years ago, when he worried that the early years policy proposals in that era were "new wine in old bottles." What he meant then was that the United States's fragmented early years *system* was not up to the task of meeting social changes like women's changing workforce participation, middle-class families wanting socialization experiences for their children, and providing compensatory learning for poor and racially minoritized children (i.e., *school readiness;* Barnett, 1993). It would be a waste of $400 billion of new wine to put it into (very) old bottles. And so this project was born.

While the issues of 1993 remain, today's consciousness and intersecting challenges demand differently conscious action. This project is forged in what some have called the "dual pandemic" (Jones, 2021). The confluence of the COVID-19 pandemic's racially disproportionate effects with the 2020 murders of Breonna Taylor, George Floyd, and Ahmaud Arbery; the uprisings for justice that followed; and our society's tolerance for mass murders in supposedly sacrosanct spaces like schools and houses of worship call attention to the indisputable fact that the early years in the United States need more than an infusion of new money or small reforms.

Structural transformation is required as a part of reparations for colonization, chattel slavery, and their living legacy (Ladson-Billings, 2006; Lloyd et al., 2021).

For the early years to be a part of national healing, we must confront the ways that racism, sexism, heteronormativity, classism, ableism, and ageism are woven into the field's policies and practices. These can be seen in preschools' assimilationist responses to immigration (Tobin et al., 2013); anti-Black punishment (Gilliam, 2005); race- and class-based early opportunity gaps (Iruka, 2020); gendered low pay (McLean et al., 2021); racial pay disparities within the field (Austin et al., 2019); negative treatment of racially minoritized students in teacher education programs (Souto-Manning et al., 2019); racial discrimination in hiring (Boyd-Swan & Herbst, 2019); and racial disproportionalities in special education (Morgan et al., 2017). These are daunting problems.

We acknowledge the impulse to say, "*I can't do anything about that. I'm just one person. I'll do what I can through my work.*" We have had these thoughts, too, but this collection draws inspiration from social movements, taking up Alan Gómez's (2016) abolitionist question, "*How do we condition the possibility of something else and decide collectively and democratically about how to get there?*" You will see how our esteemed group of early years experts responds to that question, offering many insights and concrete recommendations, but no trite answers, given these issues' complexity.

ORGANIZATION OF THE BOOK

The book is organized into seven thematic sections and a final call to collective action. Each section is made up of essays representing dialogue between the authors, which reflect varying experiences and perspectives on issues in early years policy and practice. Because this collection has so many voices, we provide brief introductions for each section to frame the issues and connect the essays. Our colleagues' biographies can be found at the end of the book.

The beginning essay in each section introduces the topic, including summarizing existing policies, their histories, and at times examples from practice, and occasionally sharing thoughts on policy proposals. The middle essays offer critiques and illustrations of how policies and systemic problems play out in the field—including how these complexities are being navigated. The sections' final essays offer recommendations and next steps for educators, researchers, advocates, and policymakers.

Given our colleagues' diversities—of perspective, role, identities, and so forth—the essays vary in their style, foci, and scope. Some take a bigger picture vantage point on the issues. Others are very personal accounts. This is intentional, as the *big* informs the *small* and vice versa—the big systems are made up of individual people, each with their own stories. This diversity of vantage points is not all-encompassing, but is an expression of the field's plurality, which is not always represented in early years research and professional literature.

OVERVIEW OF THE BOOK

Our collection opens with a section titled *Early Years Systems Fragmentation and Inequality*, which addresses how systems fragmentation must be seen in light of racial, class, and gender inequities—a theme that runs throughout the book. Lucinda Heimer begins describing the ways in which history, geography, economics, and social attitudes drew the blueprint for sharp differences that exist between early years program types, their purposes, and who has access to what. Louis Hamlyn-Harris follows by describing how this fragmented system affected his early childhood center—from funding to philosophy—and their efforts to do something about this. Jacqueline Jones ends this first section with recommendations for how this fragmented system might be made more equitable for children, their families, and their educator-caregivers.

The second section, *Centering Anti-Racism in Early Years Contexts*, foregrounds anti-racist and anti-oppressive practices that must permeate new systems, for what good are new bottles if they are filled with bad wine? Ashley J. May opens with a reflection on the existential joy that can be found in culturally grounded, racially-affirming home-based child care imbued with the power of "homeplace" (hooks, 1990). Kerry-Ann Escayg and Flóra Faragó outline proactive anti-racist practices and policies—from local centers to local, state, and federal governments—that foreground the needs and well-being of Black and other racially minoritized children and their families. Chrishana Lloyd and Julianna Carlson conclude with recommendations that are mindful of the racist and sexist history that shaped the contemporary problems of program accessibility, affordability, quality, and equity in the early years.

Within the context laid out in the first two sections, the third section, *Felt In/equities in the Early Years: Infant/Toddler Care and Education*, highlights that infant-toddler teachers are among the most marginalized members of an already marginalized field. Barbara Milner frames the state of this sector, drawing on her 30 years of experience supporting young children and their families. Emmanuelle Fincham reflects on earning a PhD while remaining a toddler teacher, bringing to the fore inequities within the field through feminist, anti-racist reflections. The section concludes with recommendations from Emily Sharrock and Annie Schaeffing for policies promoting professional recognition, equitable compensation, and better understanding of the significance of those who work with the youngest children.

Emily and Annie's recommendations lead to the next section, *De/professionalization*, which addresses how efforts to professionalize the early years, to this point, have focused more on legitimizing the field than on equity within the field. Lea Austin begins by outlining core issues and debates shaping disempowering professionalization movements in recent years. Members of the Brooklyn Coalition of Early Childhood Programs, Juliana Pinto McKeen, Fabiola Santos-Gaerlan, Alice Tse Chiu, and Wendy Jo Cole, next discuss their experiences as early years directors and how parameters set by quality improvement initiatives can paradoxically undermine their efforts to run high-quality programs. Betzaida Vera-Heredia concludes this section with recommendations for professionalization grounded in the field (vs. well-intended but often harmful top-down policies).

The fifth section, *Supporting Thriving Teachers,* builds off of Betzaida's points, providing additional illustrations of the ways professionalization can dehumanize teachers, as well as examples of ways to humanize professional spaces so that educators can thrive. Vanessa Rodriguez begins by reflecting on developing professional selfhood and the implications of what she has learned by embracing herself. Abbi Kruse shares how her philosophy for creating a nurturing early years program for both children and her staff led to the creation of an 8,000-strong group of educators who organized to survive the COVID-19 pandemic, but that has become about more than just surviving. Lori Falchi and Cristina Medellin-Paz end the section by illustrating their work helping teachers navigate systems that seem organized to keep them out of the profession, forming co-reflective relationships to help them find their professional voices.

Professionalization is a part of broader efforts to standardize the field and its practices, which is the focus of our next section, *Whose Standards?*. Alexandra Figueras-Daniel and Stephanie Curenton provide a sociopolitical-historical overview of standardization's impact on early childhood programs, viewed through the lenses of race and language. Margarita Ruiz Guerrero and Carolyn Brennan follow by inviting us to reimagine standards, curriculum, and assessment in early childhood teacher education by engaging in creative, reflective processes that acknowledge standards while also incorporating knowledge and experiences beyond these norms. The section ends with Evandra Catherine's recommendations, deeply informed by being a scholar-parent, about how standards, curricula, and assessment should be less disabling and more inclusive and expansive.

The next-to-last section, *Honoring Community Cultural Wealth*, highlights communities' often-ignored importance in both creating and undoing the inequities discussed throughout our book. Iheoma Iruka's framing essay shows how racism, sexism, and classism shape the community contexts in which people live. Importantly, her framing provides a conceptual antidote to these issues through a process of re-education, integration, critical consciousness, humility, erasure (of oppression), and reimagination (R.I.C.H.E.R.).

Jaclyn Vasquez and Mark Nagasawa next illustrate how a teacher (Jaclyn) applies her skills as an educator in community organizing centered on children's well-being. Relatedly, Eva Ruiz and Rafael Pérez-Segura's stories from their new preschool in Brooklyn, New York, provide an example of hope, aspiration, decolonization, and community integration focused on dreams of education based on relationships. Anna Lees closes this section by challenging us to dream of decolonizing our educational systems by centering on an ethics of relationality between people and the land.

The final chapter, "*Now What? Our Call to Collective Action*," draws from our colleagues' recommendations and offers beginning tools that can be used to advance these goals. We acknowledge that what we present is complex and at the same time does not include all issues affecting early years policy and practice, such as access to anti-oppressive health care, affordable housing, ableist and associated negative assumptions embedded in special education, and the near-complete absence of children's voices and perspectives on issues that concern them. Nor is the collection of voices included in this conversation as broad and inclusive as it should be.

Again, our purpose for this collection is to prompt further, and wider, action-oriented discussion about the many issues for which there are no simple answers—discussions that must include critical reflection about who has been left out and who must be a part of these actions. There will be tensions and disagreements about the path forward, and this work will feel overwhelming at times. However, we find great hope in the answers our colleagues have provided to the question, "How do we condition the possibility of something else?" Quite simply, they show us what is possible by doing it.

REFERENCES

Austin, L. J. E., Edwards, B., Chávez, R., & Whitebook, M. (2019). *Racial wage gaps in early education employment.* Center for the Study of Child Care Employment.

Barnett, W. S. (1993). New wine in old bottles. *Early Childhood Research Quarterly, 8,* 519–558.

Boyd-Swan, C., & Herbst, C. M. (2019). Racial and ethnic discrimination in the labor market for child care teachers. *Educational Researcher, 48*(7), 394–406.

Callahan, M. (2018). *Convivial research.* http://ccra.mitotedigital.org/convivialres

Gilliam, W. S. (2005, May 4). *Prekindergarteners left behind.* Yale Child Study Center.

Gómez, A. E. (2016). *The revolutionary imaginations of greater Mexico*. University of Texas Press.

hooks, b. (1990). *Yearning*. South End Press.

Iruka, I. (2020, June 22). Using a social determinants of early learning framework to eliminate educational disparities and opportunity gaps. In *Getting it right* (pp. 63–86). Foundation for Child Development.

Jones, J. M. (2021). The dual pandemics of COVID-19 and systemic racism. *School Psychology, 36*(5), 427–431.

Koch, C. (2021, November 1). *Breaking down the Build Back Better Act*. https://info.childcareaware.org/blog/breaking-down-the-build-back-better-act

Ladson-Billings, G. (2006). From the achievement gap to the education debt. *Educational Researcher, 35*(7), 3–12.

Lloyd, C. M., Carlson, J., Barnett, H., Shaw, S., & Logan, D. (2021, September). *Mary Pauper: A historical exploration of early care and education compensation, policy, and solutions*. Child Trends.

McLean, C., Austin, L. J. E., Whitebook, M., & Olson, K. L. (2021). *Early childhood workforce index 2020*. Center for the Study of Child Care Employment.

Morgan, P. L., Farkas, G., Hillemeier, M. M., & Maczuga, S. (2017). Replicated evidence of racial and ethnic disparities in disability identification in U.S. schools. *Educational Researcher, 46*(6), 305–322.

Souto-Manning, M., Buffalo, G., & Rabadi-Raol, A. (2019). Early childhood teacher certification as a site for the re-production of racial and cultural injustice. In S. A. Kessler & B. B. Swadener (Eds.), *Educating for social justice in early childhood* (pp. 46–57). Routledge.

Tobin, J. J., Arzubiaga, A., & Adair, J. K. (2013). *Children crossing borders*. Russell Sage Foundation.

Part I

EARLY YEARS SYSTEMS FRAGMENTATION AND INEQUALITY

This section sets the stage for the entire collection. Lucinda Heimer shows how the United States's famously fragmented early years system reflects the nation's racist, classist, and sexist culture and history, which creates a blueprint for inequities in the field. As a part of her framing, Lucy critiques the liberal strain in the early years profession, which does not refer to the term *liberal* as it is commonly used today, but rather the Euro-American philosophy centered on individual rights, liberty, and tensions between private-public responsibilities for social well-being. This is an important distinction to bear in mind as you engage with her essay. Louis Hamlyn-Harris follows by bringing aspects of Lucy's 10,000-foot view into sharp focus as he describes both how systems fragmentation played out in economic-racial segregation within his center and the local policymaking they did to address this. Drawing upon her extensive experience in state and federal government, Jacqueline Jones concludes with recommendations for redesigning early years systems with equity at the center.

CHAPTER 1

In This Moment . . . We Are Essential

Lucinda Heimer

The global pandemic has required us to rethink how we in the early childhood sector function as individuals within a culture of care(lessness). How are early childhood educators defined and positioned in the United States? Headlines suggest a renewed focus on the role of child care. Throughout the pandemic, early child care and education (ECE) has been deemed "essential," yet direct support for teachers caring for the youngest citizens is minimal, and thousands of centers have closed nationwide. There are 1 million fewer women in the U.S. workforce following the pandemic, illustrating the lowest female labor force participation in 30 years (Chun-Hoon, 2022). This raises the question: What role does child care play in terms of transforming education systems in the United States?

In this chapter, I review factors influencing early education systems that reinforce inequity, including the history of fragmented systems of care, definitions of care and education, and issues of public or private funding. These broad factors splinter into more complex categories that highlight inequity through biased workforce support systems and achievement gaps that continue as an education debt owed to historically marginalized children and families. The conundrum of our fragmented early years systems is not a mystery. Rather, it may be inequitable by design.

THE EARLY YEARS SYSTEM(S)

Fifty-nine percent of children ages birth to 5 are in care settings. Sixty-two percent of those children are in center care, and 20% in nonrelative home care settings (U.S. Department of Education [USDOE], 2021). However, the United States does not have a comprehensive early years system. Rather, the approach to the early years in the United States represents a confusing mixture of private, local, and state policies and programs that is shaped by beliefs that the private family bears primary responsibility for young children. This is a liberal welfare state philosophy that focuses on self-reliance and autonomy when possible, leaving care and education of the young to the family (often the mother) when possible. In addition, the United States uses a federalist approach to provision that draws on the private sector (family and community programs) and governance and funding across local, state, and federal levels (Bloch et al., 2003). While the public-private divide is evident across U.S. education systems, it is pronounced in early care and education.

- In 2018, more than twice as many children ages 3 to 5 were enrolled in public programs as compared to those in private programs. This has remained the case since the 1970s (USDOE, 2021).
- In addition, 62 universal prekindergarten (UPK) programs exist in 44 states, with just over one-third of all 4-year-olds in the country enrolled in a public program (Friedman-Krauss et al., 2021).
- Yet early years programs account for about 0.33% of the U.S. Gross Domestic Product (GDP) in 2015, while "average public spending for these costs among Organisation for Economic Co-operation and Development countries was 0.74% of GDP" (Gould & Blair, 2020, p. 3).

The lack of financial investment in the early years in the United States is profound.

Following a different regulatory procedure than public K-12 systems, early years programming is provided in both licensed and nonlicensed settings, and licensure varies by state. Care settings may include the family home, home of a nonrelative providing care, group centers, and school district sites, among others. The values and focus for early education programs may vary as well, including faith-based programs, corporate-sponsored schools, curriculum-centered schools (Montessori, Waldorf, Reggio), language immersion schools, tribal-affiliated schools, for-profit and nonprofit schools, Head Start, Birth to Three, and university laboratory preschools. Formal and informal care through family settings dominates for the birth to age 3 group (USDOE, 2021). The cost for the care, unless provided by mothers and "kith and kin" (family, friend, or neighbor), is exorbitant, and supports are limited. Preschool programming for children ages 3 to 5 is varied, including home, extended family/neighborhood care, child care centers, and more recently state and district public programs (often referred to as UPK).

Funding for care is generally provided by families. However, compensatory programs exist that provide care part-time or full-time based on income requirements, illustrating the need for financial support. State and federally funded programs for children who qualify for developmental support services through the federal Individuals with Disabilities Education Act (IDEA) provide access to education for eligible families. Eligible early education programs may also enroll families who receive child care subsidies based on income; however, doing so can require additional paperwork and coordination. This illustrates the complexity of funding, settings, and structure in early education. The history of early education programming provides a lens to better understand the potential toward equity.

RACE, CARE, AND EDUCATION

Racial narratives in early education can be traced to co-options of evolutionary theory and decades of liberal legislation enacted in the United States from the 1930s through the 1960s. In tandem, this created an environment in which whites were cared for and were also proposed as caregivers while other deserving populations were excluded or considered deficient and in need of intervention—the clearest example was Head Start. This created a racial narrative attached to care (Seiler, 2020). Head Start was the first federally funded program offering free care for young children based on income status. The majority of Head Start students (66%) identify as Black, Native American, Native Hawaiian or Pacific Islander, Asian American, or Latinx (Office of Head Start, 2019), while 62% of the workforce identifies as white (Zippia.com, 2022). Interestingly, many teachers in family care as well as assistant teachers more closely demographically represent the children. This representation incongruity at varied professional levels raises questions of who is considered expert and professional and determines the standards of professionalization. The lack of representation in the workforce reinforces the need to consider workforce development and educational support within the culturally, racially, and linguistically rich home communities of the children.

The K–12 public education system, originating with Horace Mann, was ostensibly created as an equitable system. However, U.S. public education has always been and continues to be segregated. Over 50% of the public school student population is in racially concentrated districts where over 75% of the students are either white or nonwhite (Mervosh, 2019). Therefore, the existing publicly funded K–12 education system does not offer a successful example to address equity in early years programming. In addition, though roughly 98% of children are enrolled in public kindergarten (for 5-year-olds)—kindergarten, preschool, and Head Start are segregated *by design* through racially segregated housing and residential geography. Child care deserts, in which families are left with little choice for care within close proximity, are an additional by-product of segregationist housing policies (Coates, 2014). Within all of this, the rich linguistic and cultural diversity of students is lost in translation to standardized learning and assessment common in K–12 settings that continues to push assimilation to white standard English norms.

GENDER, THE WORKFORCE, AND EQUITY

Women's rights and the care of young children are inextricably intertwined. Historically, few policies have existed to encourage women to work outside the home, and labor laws have not included child care workers. This is in contrast to policies in many other countries. The Lanham Act during World War II provided federal funds for thousands of centers specifically to support the entry of women into the workforce. These closed as the war ended, and there has not been similar funding for early years programs since. Decades later, in 1993, the Family Medical Leave Act (FMLA) was created to provide job security as parents cared for children after birth or during illness, but while the FMLA provides the right to leave, there was no additional federal or state support—leaving it to employers or as unpaid leave. More recently, during COVID, women and men were forced to leave the workforce due to reduced access to child care or lack of paid leave during illness.

How and who should fund care and education in the early years is an unresolved, centuries-old issue; the care versus education debate seeks to create hierarchies of legitimacy within the profession (Garboden Murray, 2021), as well as within the family and society. The manufactured divide between care and education in the United States originates in domestic care work as well as a liberal welfare state philosophy that focuses on the individual and private family as responsible for young children (Bloch et al., 2003). The construction of child care as mother's work while education is constructed as father's (or the school's) work also embeds the hierarchical division of emotional work from the intellectual work attributed to males or schooling outside the feminine sphere of the home.

Partially related to this historical way of reasoning, the care of young children has been underfunded and undervalued, while the education of older preschoolers and kindergarteners within school settings is currently increasingly seen as important. Since the 1960s, nearly 100% of children in the United States are in public kindergarten at age 5; however, the inequities in access, affordability, and teacher wages are rampant from birth to 4. Early care is too often viewed as a separate system only intersecting at kindergarten, with infant-toddler child care and 3- and 4-year-old care and education (preschool) largely underpaid and undervalued. A feminist ethic of care illuminates the need to explore the importance of care as synonymous with education (Ailwood et al., 2022). Stories of collaboration among early years systems and formal K–12 public systems seek to challenge the care versus education dichotomy (Heimer & Ramminger, 2020).

Centering care in the early years begins to address equity across education and social systems.

Those who care for and teach young children in the United States have been historically undervalued. Across the Pre-K–12 workforce, early childhood educators are the most racially diverse educators and the lowest paid (McLean et al., 2021). In 2020, the median hourly wage for a preschool teacher of 4-year-olds was $14.67, and for a kindergarten teacher of 5-year-olds $32.80 (McLean et al., 2021). Also, compared to K–12, this workforce, no matter where situated (e.g., type of program or geographic context), has the most women teachers or caregivers (McLean et al., 2021). This intersection of race, gender, position, and compensation for work underlines the question: What is the value of care in the United States and in its education systems? Today, in addition, the divide between care and education is accentuated by the need for credentials, or lack thereof, within the profession. For example, minimal certification is required when supporting infants and toddlers. However, bachelor's degrees and licenses are required for teachers in "formal" or publicly funded K–12 and universal pre-K classrooms. Is it possible to raise the status of the workforce as highly valued caring professionals without mirroring our current education system with a required need for credentials? Credentials serve a purpose, but also exclude populations of teachers and set up a hierarchy. Divisions in early years education are manufactured and counterproductive.

FRAGMENTATION TO INTERSECTIONS

To teach in a manner that respects and cares for the souls of our students is essential if we are to provide the necessary conditions where learning can most deeply and intimately begin (hooks, 1994, p. 13). These ideas support our workforce, families, and children in navigating centuries-long systems of oppression. Drilling below the surface of education systems to discover the soul of a caring society provides possibility. In addition, greater attention to the importance of both care and education—which are both occurring from infancy onward—could heighten respect and a revaluing of care in the early years. This then would begin to address broad issues of equity across both education and social systems. International studies of early education systems have raised the need for basic structures, including (a) a strong policy foundation; (b) comprehensive services, funding, and governance; (c) knowledgeable and supported teachers and families; (d) informed, individualized, and continuous pedagogy; and (e) data to drive improvement (Kagan, 2019).

These considerations offer promise for addressing fragmented and misunderstood early education and care systems. However, the soul of early education depends on our willingness to address how we have come to this moment of inequity. There is a *desire* to fund solutions through potential legislation totaling $400 billion for child care and preschool (Build Back Better), but no action at this time, as at many other junctures of the past. Reframing U.S. educational history may not be enough; rather, walking through recent health, social, and political global crises may provide the perspective needed to work toward, pay for, explore, and inform what is possible in the early years in uncertain times.

This brief review illustrates an early years system designed to fail and offers hope to consider new ways to fund early years programs, improve representation of diverse demographics, equitably compensate the early years workforce, and align programing in a way that honors individual experience. The following chapter highlights the power in our personal stories through one example of the public-private conundrum, and the section concludes with early years systems recommendations. The intersection of past and present systems illuminates next steps.

REFERENCES

Ailwood, J., Lee, I-F., Arndt, S., Tesar, M., Aslanian, T., Gibbons, A., & Heimer, L. (2022). Communities of care. *Policy Futures in Education.* Advance online publication. https://doi.org/10.1177/14782103211064440

Bloch, M. N., Holmlund, K., Moqvist, I., & Popkewitz, T. (2003). Global and local patterns of governing the child, family, their care, and education. In M. N. Bloch, K. Holmlund, I. Molqvist, I., & T. Popkewitz (Eds.) *Governing children, families and education* (pp. 3–34). Palgrave Press.

Chun-Hoon, W. (February 27, 2022). *A federal conversation.* NAEYC Policy Summit Presentation. National Association for the Education of Young Children.

Coates, T. (2014, June). The case for reparations. *The Atlantic.* https://www .theatlantic.com/magazine/archive/2014/06/the-case-for-reparations/361631/

Friedman-Krauss, A., Barnett, W. S., Garver, K. A., Hodges, K. S., Weisenfeld, G. G., & Gardiner, B. (2021). *The state of preschool 2020.* National Institute for Early Education Research.

Garboden Murray, C. (2021). *Illuminating care.* Exchange Press.

Gould, E., & Blair, H. (2020). *Who's paying now?* Economic Policy Institute.

Heimer, L. G., & Ramminger, A. E. (2020). *Reshaping universal preschool.* Teachers College Press.

hooks, b. (1994). *Teaching to transgress.* Routledge.

Kagan, S. L. (2019). *The early advantage 2.* Teachers College Press.

McLean, C., Austin, L. J. E., Whitebook, M., & Olson, K. L. (2021). *Early childhood workforce index 2020.* Center for the Study of Child Care Employment, University of California, Berkeley.

Mervosh, S. (February 27, 2019). How much wealthier are white school districts than nonwhite ones? $23 billion, report says. *The New York Times.*

https://www.nytimes.com/2019/02/27/education/school-districts-funding
-white-minorities.html

Office of Head Start. (2019). *Head Start program facts: Fiscal year 2019.*

Seiler, C. (2020). White origins of care. *Social Text, 142*(38), 17–38.

U.S. Department of Education. (2021). *Early childhood program participation: 2019* (NCES 2020-075REV). National Center for Education Statistics. https://nces.ed.gov/pubsearch/pubsinfo.asp?pubid=2020075REV

Zippia.com. (2022, April 18). *Head Start teacher demographics and statistics in the U.S.* https://www.zippia.com/head-start-teacher-jobs/demographics/

CHAPTER 2

One Center, Two Programs
Finding Promise Within a Fragmented and Unequal Non-System

Louis Hamlyn-Harris

In 2016, I took a leadership position in the early childhood department of a historic community center on New York City's Lower East Side. That department turned out to consist of two separate programs, operating in tandem since the mid-1960s: one funded mostly by tuition fees, and the other by Head Start and Early Head Start. Bringing them together required navigating deeply held assumptions about the value of integration and the purpose of early childhood education.

Our fee-based preschool was typical of those in its price range in our city. Inspired by the schools of Reggio Emilia, teachers observed children closely, looking for the deep themes and common patterns of their questions, interests, and theories. They built curriculum around abstractions like "fairness," "transformation," or "community" and encouraged children to express their ideas using clay, wire, and found materials. The preschool was considered a social lifeline for new parents, but despite our rhetoric of diversity, most families came from the largely racially and economically homogeneous co-ops surrounding the park we visited for outside play (co-ops are apartment buildings that are owned cooperatively by residents, who are often relatively affluent).

To increase access, we offered financial aid, which became an annual ritual of projection and heartbreak; despite ever-increasing requests, we never managed to offer more than a small discount on tuition rates we knew excluded many in the community. Exclusion also operated in other, more subtle ways. Though we'd become skilled at accommodating children with developmental differences, we offered few supports to families seeking stability, and we felt powerless when children presented symptoms of crisis or trauma.

Conversely, our Head Start program was academically traditional, with a focus on skills acquisition and school readiness. The latter was defined rather narrowly by preliteracy and numeracy exercises that teachers shared and adapted to their age groups. Classrooms were divided into stations, each clearly labeled with their intended (and, usually, exclusive) purpose. Guidelines shaded imperceptibly into rules and, ultimately, mythologies— for example, timely drop-off was enforced through an inflexible late pass system, and there was a widely enforced understanding that Head Start didn't allow glass in classrooms.

Despite these strictures, many of the teachers were among the kindest, most generous people I'd ever met. Their practices were trauma-informed and culturally responsive. Many spoke Chinese and Spanish, common home languages in our community. In-house social work, mental health, and social services departments provided professional development to teachers and resources like counseling, play therapy, and English classes to families. Parents, many of whom were steeped in the activist traditions of our neighborhood, sat on the parent policy council, planned community events, and formed a partnership with the local credit union.

SEGREGATED SYSTEMS = SEGREGATED PROGRAMS

These two programs—let's call them private and public—were administered, budgeted, and operated completely separately; our CEO was the only common link in our organization chart. Each program offered universal prekindergarten (UPK), funded by the city and free of charge, but because returning families received the highest enrollment preference, the makeup of these classrooms was little different from the earlier ages. To no one's surprise, children graduating from them went into two nonoverlapping sets of local public schools, stratified in terms of demographics, social services, and test scores. Despite sharing physical space, children, families, and staff had few opportunities to make decisions together or build relationships across lines of difference. This arrangement, which we sometimes experienced as an individual failure of courage, was actually completely typical—that year our city's school system was rated the second-most segregated in the country. When we went looking for examples of successful integration under similar conditions, we found none.

When we were asked about the separation (which happened frequently), we gave the official answer: Our funding partners didn't speak to one another and, absent their cooperation, braiding funding was complicated and risky. To add to the challenge, Head Start gave us less than two-thirds of our already tight tuition rates per seat, and these dollars had to stretch considerably further to cover additional expenses and functions required by the performance standards. Accordingly, teachers in Head Start earned significantly less than their private peers and typically had fewer formal qualifications. Then there was the regulatory burden—a truly integrated program would have to reconcile requirements from the local departments of health and education as well as federal Head Start, without guidance or forgiveness if a mistake was made.

Divergent Evolution

These issues are real and without obvious solutions, but I felt that this conversation masked more profound differences between the two models. Put simply, our private and public programs had evolved into two independent paradigms that operated on different assumptions about the role and purpose of early education. The fragmentation extended beyond regulations and funding models and had become discursive, aesthetic, and ethical. This created dilemmas for us integrationists that I don't see reflected in our policy debates:

- As a field, what are our core values and principles?
- What commitments do we make to children?
- To what extent are differentiated approaches and methods justified by differences in families' needs and circumstances?
- When we create something new, whose language and histories do we employ and honor? Who is asked to step out of their comfort zone? Who gets to choose?

The truth was, our public and private systems more generally had little shared vocabulary or history of exchange, and their visions of what early childhood education is and does didn't align easily. Take the issue of school choice. Children in our private program typically went on to progressive public elementary schools. Their teachers and parents understood that imagination, curiosity, and a willingness to challenge authority would be valued in those environments, which had the effect of liberating the children from the demands of the future—the language of *preparation* and *readiness* was rarely used, and assessing children's learning had little urgency beyond informing immediate planning.

Head Start, on the other hand, is relentlessly teleological: children are perceived as at risk of *falling behind* and in need of *catching up*—crisis logic that demands targeted intervention. Strengths-based language often masks images of children grounded in ideas of paucity, poverty, and delay. For these children, the future is always present. One word for all of this is privilege: Our private program had the autonomy to relax, experiment, and let children make their own meaning, largely unburdened by administrative overload or curriculum standards. In illustrative contrast, the word "requirement" appears 147 times in the Head Start Performance Standards; "play" appears just seven times.

Unequal Childhoods Under One Roof

Living and working under this model also had an affective dimension. Segregation made people deeply, viscerally uncomfortable. Families would bring it up on tours and teachers discussed it constantly. There was a general understanding that our children were spending their formative years—the time their identities and maps of the world are formed—under conditions of separation. Our explanations offended people's moral senses. Proximity heightened the contradictions to an unbearable level; the usual means by which we explain away or overlook inequality felt untenable when children's experience was determined so clearly by which button they pressed on the elevator. The challenges posed by integration were considerable, but our community's energy for change presented an opportunity to jump in and figure out the details as we went.

A COLLECTIVE LEAP OF FAITH

At first, jumping in meant collaborating more intentionally. We planned joint professional development and community events: sing-alongs, family arts workshops, playdates, and volunteer opportunities. Like any collaboration, this process was alternately exciting and frustrating. Importantly, it forced us to grapple with and reconcile many of our unspoken assumptions, expectations, and priorities, often to productive ends (one professional development day included a workshop on adverse childhood experiences as well as a metaphor-rich clay experience involving bridge-building). Ultimately, we realized that though the relationships we'd built would serve us well, collaboration and integration are two different muscles. The next phase would require structural change.

We agreed on a pilot—four classrooms of children entering kindergarten the following year. Teachers from both programs were invited to write a short statement of interest to apply; many did, despite basic details being unconfirmed. We suspected that families across the socioeconomic spectrum shared some important goals for their children, but our experience had taught us not to assume we all used the same vocabulary. So we decided that our pilot classrooms would be loudly and self-consciously progressive. We met with incoming families to reflect on our own upbringings and talk about concepts like autonomy, choice, assessment, and play. Our teachers made a big investment in pedagogical documentation, which they used to surface children's interests and prior knowledge but also to communicate our seriousness to families and present alternatives to numerical assessment tools.

We made an effort to pair teachers who'd previously worked in different programs and carved out space—always too little—for regular reflective conversations. These pairings weren't frictionless—teachers disagreed frequently about planning methods, the role of the teacher, and tolerance for risk. Sorting out assessment and curriculum was a big challenge; we successfully advocated for an emergent curriculum to replace the off-the-shelf tools we'd inherited, but only after much experimentation with hybrid models that exhausted our teachers.

We shared the resources and services we'd developed in our Head Start program with all families and tried to think of ways to also honor their contributions, experimenting with structures like storytelling sessions and parenting groups that gave participants a chance to give as well as receive support. We extended drop-off time longer to encourage lingering and suspended the late pass system; family engagement as an end in itself, rather than a means to teach skills or *lift families out of poverty*, required a shift in thinking for some of our staff.

We spent months exploring the kindergarten admissions process together, working with school principals and the local department of education to offer workshops, group tours, and debrief sessions. Families who were exposed to inspired classrooms bought in, and concerns about the new approach dissipated quickly. But community-building is a slow and messy process. We learned not to assume that only middle-class families would be discomfited by the changes associated with integration. The pilot wasn't perfect, but it created a sense of inevitability—our community would no longer accept *separate but equal*.

A PROMISING BEGINNING

In 2020, after more than 50 years of separation, we fully integrated our early childhood programs. That August, we created teaching teams and classroom assignments based on schedules and goodness of fit—for the first time, children's funding source was only a matter for the finance team. This marked the start of a journey that I lack the space to summarize here. Suffice it to say, integrating a preschool doesn't erase inequality or resolve larger social divisions, though it's probably not a bad place to start. Our model remains unfamiliar to governments, and financial sustainability requires a braided-funding model that could be revoked at any time. As a staff, we're learning and growing, constantly negotiating and trying to reconcile the demands of the public and private paradigms.

Despite all that, the most remarkable thing about our integrated preschool might be its ordinariness. Administrators worry about funding. Teachers navigate the complexities and dilemmas of the planning cycle. Families bond over common experiences of sleepless nights and sibling rivalry. Above all, children are children. Who ever thought otherwise?

CHAPTER 3

Toward Transforming Fragmented and Unequal Early Years Systems— Recommendations

Jacqueline Jones

Over the past 50 years, a growing body of research across several domains of knowledge has influenced public policy related to the field of early child care and education (ECE) (Jones & Vecchiotti, 2020). When the Head Start program began in the 1960s, there was little publicly funded center-based care available to young preschool-aged children living in poor and low-income households. Significant advances have occurred with the major focus on expansion of preschool services.

Head Start has expanded to include Early Head Start for infants and toddlers, 44 states support some type of preschool programming (Friedman-Krauss et al., 2021), and private providers of preschool programming have expanded their reach. There has been widespread recognition of the benefits of preschool (Phillips et al., 2017; Yoshikawa et al., 2013) as increased numbers of working women have required child care for their children. Yet, as Lucy and Louis have outlined, the field continues to be challenged by fragmented funding streams and inequalities within the early years workforce. This section offers recommendations for the public and private sector to move the field toward coherence, a deeper sense of equity, and stronger outcomes for all children.

A NEW SYSTEM

There is little doubt that if we could create a new system of early child care and education for the United States, it would look quite different from the one that has evolved over the past 50-plus years. The field functions as a fragmented set of funding streams rather than as a coherent system designed to support a strong pipeline of informed and curious citizens. The major federal programs, the Child Care Development Block Grant

(CCDBG), Head Start, Title I of the Every Student Succeeds Act, and the Individuals with Disabilities Education Act (IDEA), function independently of each other, are authorized separately, and are operated across the federal Departments of Education and Health and Human Services. Except for the Head Start program, whose funds flow directly from the federal government to community programs, other federal funds go through state governments to communities. The result, as Louis described, is a system that interacts with children and families based on the funding stream to which they are attached. Community programs are left to "blend" and "braid" federal, state, and local funding in order to provide services to children and families (Jones, 2018).

Fragmentation of the early years sector is now the status quo, and real change is challenging. Meaningful transformation requires a reconceptualization of how we view young children, what kind of people we want them to become, and society's role and responsibility in nurturing them. A new system would move beyond compensatory interventions for young children who have been described over the years as culturally, linguistically, and economically deprived, disadvantaged, deficient, and limited. A new system would adopt what Hilliard (1996) referred to several decades ago as a *human metaphor.*

From this perspective, *all* children are viewed as meaning-makers, trying to figure out how the world works and how to communicate their needs and wishes. Regardless of linguistic, racial, ethnic, or economic status, their individual, family, and community assets are acknowledged and affirmed. Federal, state, and local agencies work in partnership with families and communities to ensure that each child reaches their full potential. A reconceptualization of early years systems would ensure that children who are most likely to face academic underachievement receive the same types of exploratory, inquiry-based, active learning experiences as their wealthier peers. In addition, this model would create the conditions that could enable the preparation, appropriate compensation, and ongoing support of a diverse cadre of skilled professionals who demonstrate a keen understanding of how children learn and the practices that facilitate and promote optimal development for all children (Falk, 2018).

A new system would provide families with access to a suite of supports, including Child and Dependent Care Tax Credit (CDCTC), Earned Income Tax Credit (EITC), Supplemental Nutrition Assistance Program (SNAP), paid family leave, affordable high-quality universal early child care and education beginning at birth, center- and home-based universal early child care, and universal high-quality full-day kindergarten. In this new model, children and families get what they need and are oblivious to the background sources of funding for individual services. High-quality, culturally affirming early years services are available to all children and families; children are not defined by the funding streams for which they are eligible. Policies ensure that the professionals who provide early years services have mastered the requisite competencies, are appropriately compensated, and receive the ongoing supports needed to perform at high levels.

RECOMMENDATIONS: EARLY YEARS FUNDING FRAGMENTATION

Because funding fragmentation originates at the federal level, the federal government should make efforts to streamline early years funding to states and community-based programs (Jones, 2018). The boldest action would be consolidation of all, or at least the major, federal programs that support young children under one federal office. This office could be housed in either the Department of Education or Health and Human Services, or in a newly formed department solely dedicated to the learning and development of young children. Several states have already attempted to coordinate early years services (Connors-Tadros et al., 2021); it is time for federal government coordination.

Federal Recommendations

- In the absence of complete consolidation of early years programs, the federal government could align the major funding streams across teacher qualifications, eligibility criteria, compliance parameters, and so on. Each reauthorization should consider how the program aligns with the other sources of support for children and families.
- The increase in state and locally funded early childhood programs requires greater flexibility linking to federal funds. Greater alignment would facilitate a true mixed delivery system in which multiple funds, such as Head Start and state preschool, could be pooled under a single set of programmatic, fiscal, and compliance standards, providing high-quality early years services to the maximum number of children and families.

Private-Sector Recommendations

- Fund states and localities to pilot and disseminate effective strategies to coordinate funding.
- Fund a National Academies of Sciences, Engineering, and Medicine (NASEM) consensus study to generate recommendations for federal, state, and local coordination of early years program funding.

RECOMMENDATIONS: EARLY YEARS WORKFORCE

A strong pipeline of well-prepared and appropriately compensated early years professionals who reflect the diversity of the communities in which they work does not develop by chance. Simply requiring a degree or credential, or renaming categories of professionals, will not address issues of equity, access to high-quality preparation, appropriate compensation, and ongoing support. In addition, the persistent low compensation for high numbers of Black and brown women raises social justice issues and threatens to destabilize an already fragile system. There are significant compensation disparities across settings, such as Head Start, private providers, and public schools, with the highest salary and benefits in the public schools. Compensation and preparation disparities also exist across the birth–3, preschool, and K–3 age groups, with teachers of infants and toddlers receiving significantly less compensation than preschool or K–3 teachers (Whitebook et al., 2014).

While these inequities exist, the system will remain destabilized, and as teachers improve their skills and earn more credentials, they will seek preschool and K–3 positions in order to feed their families. Further, the inequalities in compensation and support have the potential to put children at risk. As stated in the *Transforming the Workforce* report, ". . . adults who are under informed, underprepared, or subject to chronic stress themselves may contribute to children's experiences of adversity and stress and undermine their development and learning" (Institute of Medicine [IOM], 2015, p. 4). While these recommendations are complex, they would help to remove inequities and acknowledge the experience and knowledge of our current workforce, which would not only help to maintain the workforce, but also grow it.

Federal Government Recommendations

- Across federal early years programs, at a minimum, require qualifications that include a solid foundation in child development, a variety of student teaching experiences, a research base on the role of culture in teaching and learning, and strategies to establish meaningful partnerships with families.
- Ensure that historically Black colleges and universities (HBCUs) and Hispanic- and Native-serving institutions are sufficiently funded to develop and sustain high-quality early years teacher preparation programs.
- Forgive student loans for early childhood teachers, especially for those who are not even being paid at parity with their public school peers. Existing programs that assist early years professionals in financing their education, such as TEACH, should be funded to expand their reach.

- Fund higher education programs to cover completely, or significantly defray, tuition costs for students enrolled in early years teacher preparation programs.
- Reward eligible higher education institutions for actively recruiting candidates who reflect the cultural diversity of the country.

State and Local Recommendations

- Actively recruit teachers who reflect the ethnic, linguistic, and cultural characteristics of the communities in which they teach.
- Provide teachers in Head Start and private provider settings with compensation comparable to public school teachers with equivalent credentials and experience.
- Provide all early years teachers with ongoing professional learning that reflects the current science of early development with attention to equity and cultural diversity.

Early Childhood Field and Private-Sector Recommendations

- Support higher education institutions to redesign their early years programs to be grounded in current research on child development, support successful learning and development for all children, and include both the theory and clinical practice of early learning and development.
- Support the development and adoption of a nationally agreed-upon set of early years educator competencies that serve as the foundation to create a national early years certification. Such a certification would be portable across states and accepted as meeting the criteria for state licensing. Financial support must be provided to cover any certification fee; increases in compensation must be triggered when the certification is awarded.
- The public does not appear to be convinced that the work of educating young children has a solid and complex academic and clinical foundation and requires skilled professionals. It's time for a national public awareness campaign that can change the narrative around the early years, underscore the importance of the work, and highlight the complex set of competencies that must be mastered.

Yes, these recommendations are expensive, but maintaining the status quo may be more costly to everyone (National Academies of Sciences, Engineering, and Medicine, 2018). Let's create a system that works.

REFERENCES

Connors-Tadros, L., Northey, K., Freede, E., Hodges, K., & Jost, T. (2021). *Effective state offices of early learning*. National Institute for Early Education Research (NIEER).

Falk, B. (2018). *High-quality early learning for a changing world*. Teachers College Press.

Friedman-Krauss, A. H., Barnett, W. S., Garver, K. A., Hodges, K. S., Weisenfeld, G. G., & Gardiner, B. A. (2021). *The state of preschool 2020*. National Institute for Early Education Research (NIEER).

Hilliard, A. G. (1996). Maintaining the Montessori metaphor. *North American Montessori Teachers Association, 21*(9), 108–125.

Institute of Medicine (IOM), National Research Council (NRC). (2015). *Transforming the workforce for children birth through 8*. The National Academies Press.

Jones, J. (2018). U.S. early childhood policy. In L. Miller, C. Cameron, C. Dalli, & N. Barbour (Eds.), *The Sage handbook of early childhood policy* (pp. 133–150). Sage Publications.

Jones, J., & Vecchiotti, S. (2020). Policy and political influences on early childhood education. In D. F. Gullo & M. E. Graue, (Eds.), *Scientific influences on early childhood education* (pp. 37–54). New York: Routledge.

National Academies of Sciences, Engineering, and Medicine. (2018). *Transforming the financing of early care and education*. The National Academies Press.

Phillips, D. A., Lipsey, M. W., Dodge, K. A., Haskins, R., Bassok, D., Burchinal, M. R., Duncan, G. J., Dynarski, M., Magnuson, K. A., & Weiland, C. (2017). Puzzling it out: The current state of scientific knowledge on pre-k effects. In K. A. Dodge, R. Haskins, M. W. Lipsey, and D. A. Phillips (Eds.), *The current state of scientific knowledge on pre-kindergarten effects* (pp. 19–30). Brookings Institution and Duke Center for Child and Family Policy.

Whitebook, M., Phillips, D. A., & Howes, C. (2014). *Worthy work, still unlivable wages*. Center for the Study of Child Care Employment.

Yoshikawa, H., Weiland, C., Brooks-Gunn, J., Burchinal, M., Espinosa, L., Gormley, W. T., Ludwig, J., Magnuson, K., Phillips, D., & Zaslow, M. (2013). *Investing in our future*. http://fcd-us.org/resources/evidence-base-preschool

Part II

CENTERING ANTI-RACISM IN EARLY YEARS CONTEXTS

What has been referred to as the "three-legged stool" of early years programming, comprising accessibility, affordability, and quality, offers a metaphor for the precarity as well as the possibilities for a more inclusive, holistic, and universally accessible system. This section foregrounds the critical dimension of equity and explicitly anti-oppressive practices, with focus on anti-racist possibilities. Authors in this section engage with nuanced issues of culture, care, and systems that variously support—or undermine—care for children, families, and early educators. Ashley J. May reflects powerfully on kith and kin care serving as a cultural and linguistic home space. Kerry-Ann Escayg and Flóra Faragó elucidate proactive anti-racist practices and propose policies—from child care centers to state— that foreground the needs and well-being of Black and other racialized children and their families. Asking critical questions and providing concrete examples, they provide rich examples from research and practice. Chrishana Lloyd and Julianna Carlson conclude with recommendations that frame the critical contexts of accessibility, affordability, quality, and equity in the early years. Their call to action and policy recommendations engage the many provocations raised by the authors in this section and offer a powerful vision for the future of early years in the United States.

CHAPTER 4

Constellations of Care

Black Kith and Kin Home/Place-Making Beyond the State Gaze

Ashley J. May

> The undoing of the plot begins with her drifting from the course, with an errant path, with getting lost to the world. The undoing begins with an escape to the woods, with perilous freedom, with petit maroonage, with wading in the water. It does not begin with proclamations or constitutions or decrees or appeals or a seat at the table or a stake in the game.
>
> —Saidiya Hartman (2022, "The Plot of Her Undoing" in *Notes on Feminisms*)

Together, under a canopy of lush, green trees, I gathered with Syrian mothers and children mobilized in the work of living liberated Muslim childhood futures, now, in Los Angeles, California. Over tea, my co-dreamers professed their love for a Syrian auntie at the center of their network of care. She made a home away from homelands for the children of this close-knit Syrian community, wanting hardly anything in exchange. The mothers returned their children to her care again and again to remember, together, what they feared losing hold of in the wake of displacement: tradition, food, language, and the care of an elder who reminded them of homelands, in spite of the oceans between them.

This model of care felt familiar. My own mother chose a place of affirmation, shared culture, language, and protection for me. While pregnant in 1979, she worked for Watts Labor Community Action Committee. In anticipation of her return to work, she gathered caregiver recommendations via communal networks and word of mouth. My grandmother did the same.

Eventually, they found Earlene. Earlene was a relative of my grandmother's co-worker. She was a mother already staying home with her own child; he was just about a year older than I was. Earlene got great joy caring for me while my mother worked. At the end of the day, Earlene welcomed my mother with a smiling baby and a plate of food—a bit of home away from home; a very Southern thing and a very common ethic of care extended by Black folks more broadly. And for the next 4 years or so, until I entered formal preschool, I would be *at home* with Earlene on most days, on other days my grandparents, and on occasion with an auntie. A network of my kith and kinfolk that mapped out over home, place, and time to form what I refer to as a constellation of care—a practice of place-making that registers as both radical imaginary and what has always already existed in order for us to survive. An errant path. An inward turn. Something like celestial plottings toward a guiding star, one neither entirely visible nor legible; something we must take care to witness.

I move deliberately from memories of working with Syrian mothers and children to several conversations over time with my mother about our constellation of care not simply to frame this as a story about myself, but to situate myself within this work; to place us, all these other constellations of care that have mapped across time and place, together in the wake of Black dispossession, displacement, and the afterlife of slavery.

In Christina Sharpe's *In the Wake: On Blackness and Being* (2016), she defines *wake* as "the track left on the water's surface by a ship; the disturbance caused by a body swimming or moved in water; it is the air currents behind a body in flight; a region of disturbed flow" (p. 3). I move along this wake with Black homeplace as my unit of observation and I ask: How might we shift our ways of thinking about Black homeplace and the care that *takes place* within its boundaries? How have Black families, and those who care for them, insisted on life beyond the state and its policies on kith and kin care? And how might those decision-making practices be mobilized into transformation?

I offer here a set of provocations for imagining otherwise, rending the false alliance of statecraft with Black homeplace. A rerouting from the carceral logic of monitoring and compliance toward the possibility in the fugitive homeplace. A place where ways of an unbound loving, caring for, and protecting Black children serve as evidence of living through the wake. A cultural artifact, I suppose, that transforms enclosures lurking in early years policy. To move into this provocation, I first locate Black homeplace as a sanctuary of care central to this argument. Then, I offer a discussion of kith and kin care in Black homeplace-making as a practice of fugitivity—turning the lens on the state and its allies, naming the ways in which it acts to form a system that is already always oriented toward Black death. And, finally, I chart pathways for imagining otherwise, a straying off of the course as it stands, toward a new world where the system as we know it can no longer thrive.

WHERE CARE TAKES PLACE

It is through bell hooks's (1990) theorizing on Black homeplace that I began to think about Black kith and kin care and place-making as the fruit of a radical imaginary. hooks's concept of homeplace affirms, restores, and acts as refuge from the violence and hardship of the outside world (1990, p. 42). And it is here that I argue Black kith and kin care *takes place*. Not only as a practice of resistance, as hooks offers, but also as a site of care and sanctuary.

This is a critical shift in terms key to conceptualizing the power of the Black homeplace to shape the way statecraft moves through us, those with a stake in the game, to extend care to/for kith and kin care. I wish to trouble the impulse of statecraft to contain kith and kin caregivers, but specifically Black kith and kin caregivers, to the provision of service. Thinking through the power of the quotidian and its usefulness beyond a universal labor in service to the state, subject to determinations of quality and translatability, is the positioning of Black homeplace in and of the wake. Rather, as an insistence on living un/imaginable lives in the face of Black dispossession, the unfinished project of emancipation (Sharpe, 2016), and a refusal of statecraft in order to build something otherwise.

> If you are providing care and supervision to children without a license in a home or facility that is not license-exempt you need to understand that you are breaking the law. Operating without a license is a misdemeanor and subject to a $200 per day fine. You may also be subject to criminal charges by local law enforcement. (California Department of Social Services, 2022)

The state's impulse to surveil and enclose upon the Black homeplace is carceral logic in action. Statecraft writ large insists on criminalizing this literal lifesaving practice of fugitivity. Here, refusal to take up license regulations or engage with state-crafted solutions is to be in opposition to the law—and therefore insisting on life in a system oriented toward Black death. Black fugitive homeplace-making is a quotidian refusal—quiet, but not silent—demanding our attention (Campt, 2014).

Through crafting homeplace beyond this carceral gaze, kith and kin constellations of care rupture systems of compliance between the state and its subjects, requiring that we look and listen in unlikely places for the quiet, quotidian practices of refusal that must exist, that are requisite for a radical remaking of this world. Anecdotal testimony from fieldwork jottings and deep listening on the ground, as well as numerous technical reports that speak to the difficulties faced engaging kith and kin caregivers, ask us to operationalize a tool not often utilized—to love and to listen to the ruptures in the terms of this relationship between Black homeplace and the state.

PLOTTING NEW DIRECTIONS, TOGETHER

Along this path to imagining otherwise, I return to the following questions: How might the state enter into careful conversation with the fugitive Black homeplace? Fugitivity doesn't always register on a survey; the language of refusal only reveals so much in a focus group. How can the state and its allies arrive at the sort of question-mapping critical for the unveiling of uncomfortable truths? Not for the sake of making Black homeplace more legible, but to sift out from this rich soil a list of demands needed to imagine something better than the current state of affairs. A place where fines, penalties, and other carceral reflexes in opposition of Black life, self-determination, and the radical care of children can no longer thrive. I propose a way forward rooted in deep listening as love (Shange, 2019), collective study, and moving together in political struggle (James, 2021) as a path worth taking so that we might grow something new.

We as folks working in the care of Black kith and kin caregivers must agitate statecraft by sharpening our own tools of relationality, in order that we come to understand fugitivity as sanctuary in the face of enclosure, as meaning-making we should take care to listen to, not as a failure to comply with the state. We can carry on business as usual, with this carceral reflex moving through our bodies as we push out programs that barely move toward transformation and keep us veiled from what's really, really going on in the community. Or we can choose otherwise by getting down on the ground in radical love for those we serve.

Policy alone won't bring forth the kind of liberation we are after. It is nothing more than the compromise of the state, an alleged love for a community that never quite moves down (James, 2021). So we must get on the ground, together with communities and their demands, in order to build the world we wish to make (James, 2021; Shange, 2019), to strategize, to agitate from the inside out. What does that look like?

It looks like sitting together with kith and kin caregivers, to listen, to imagine what this world could look like if we moved away from the criminalization of Black women and children, if we operated first from a trust, without the looming threat of surveillance. And getting there takes work. The work of divesting from systems that render communities disposable, that focus on basic needs with no consideration for their political desires (James, 2021). How can we make a claim to care for them without understanding what's eating at the roots of their communities: dispossession, gentrification, and displacement? I do not mean to imply that liberation is achieved by simply eradicating economic precarity—the path to liberation is a complex struggle.

Together *with* them, not *for* them, is how we move forward in struggle with Black kith and kin caregivers, children, and families *in place*. From this, concrete demands emerge to light our path forward toward transformation, without enclosing on the rebellion, the radical insistence to survive in the wake. In relationship with the Black homeplace, we build, not destroy, the rich soil for self-determination and transform material conditions instead of criminalizing precarity. We dare to exist, in the care of one another, beyond the gaze of the state, too. And this takes an unbound imagination.

REFERENCES

California Department of Social Services. (2022). *Resources for parents: Types of child care in California. The STATE CDSS Law on LE/FFN.* https://www.cdss.ca.gov/inforesources/child-care-licensing/resources-for-parents

Campt, T. M. (2014, October). *Black feminist futures and the practice of fugitivity.* Lecture presented at the Helen Pond McIntyre '48 Lecture at the Barnard Center for Research on Women, New York, NY.

Hartman, S. (2022). *The plot of her undoing.* https://feministartcoalition.org/essays-list/saidiya-hartman

hooks, b. (1990). *Yearning.* South End Press.

James, J. (2021, January). Captive maternal love and war stories. *Ethics, Aesthetics, Feminisms,* 2021 C4E Journal. https://c4ejournal.net/2021/01/22/joy-james-captive-maternal-love-and-war-stories-ethics-aesthetics-feminisms-2021-c4ej-4/

Shange, S. (2019). *Progressive dystopia.* Duke University Press.

Sharpe, C. (2016). *In the wake: On Blackness and being.* Duke University Press.

CHAPTER 5

Proactive, Not Reactive

Creating Anti-Racist Policies for Child Care Centers and Preschools

Kerry-Ann Escayg and Flóra Faragó

The recent advent of anti-racist pedagogical approaches in the early years sector signals a shift toward identifying covert and overt expressions of racism in classrooms and child care centers. Calls for early child care and education (ECE) to undergo a structural transformation have begun to initiate change, foregrounding the well-being of Black and racialized children. The overarching principles of anti-racism challenge how Eurocentric perspectives—undergirded by white privilege and power—inform research, perceptions of children, policy, teaching and learning practices, and the critical knowledge base of the early years profession. In this chapter, we explore the interrelated processes of developing anti-racist policies specific to preschool and child care contexts.

Given the undue impact of systemic racism over the lived realities of Black, Indigenous, and People of Color (BIPOC), the development of an anti-racist early childhood policy at both municipal and national levels plays an essential role in transforming the early years. Research on anti-racist early years national policy is limited, aside from a few peer-reviewed critical maps charting the development and implementation of anti-racist policies aimed at reconceptualizing and reforming the field (exceptions include Escayg, 2019; Iruka et al., 2021; Minoff et al., 2020). Policymaking directs institutional, collective, and individual action on the explicitly anti-racist goal of racial equity by supporting, protecting, and honoring Black and racialized children of intersecting social identities.

While substantial scholarship acknowledges how racism, and in particular, anti-Black racism, operates concurrently with the enduring economic corollaries of European colonialism and chattel slavery, for the current analysis, consideration is restricted to early years systems in Canada and the United States. This chapter shares strategies for utilizing anti-racist frameworks in child care centers and preschools, by identifying the requisite components—terminologies, procedures, and so on—essential to cultivating an anti-racist learning space and, by extension, an anti-racist organizational culture grounded in an awareness of the social dimensions of racism. This essay allows for integrative anti-racist practices in the early years, including positive family-centered relationships. Concluding sections discuss the benefits of anti-racist policies for children, educators, and the early childhood field. By way of creative expressions, most notably, a self-reflective dialogue, the authors provide a brief narrative that elucidates their personal trajectories as early childhood scholars and advocates for racial justice.

Flóra: Kerry-Ann, what brought you to the field of anti-racism in ECE?

Kerry-Ann: Flóra, that's a good question. In retrospect, I believe it was a path I was always called to—a divine destiny, if you will. Growing up in Trinidad and experiencing the vestiges of colonial rule in my early years certainly shaped my consciousness around race and racial identity. Conversely, moving to Canada in my teens, and attending college and university, provided the learning experiences—the rich experiential material—by which I was able to decolonize—to come into the fullness of an anti-colonial/decolonized identity. I characterize the process as a spiritual awakening, a rebirth. Indeed, such was and remains the foundation for my anti-racist and pan-African scholarship.

As the Word says, "And a child shall lead them." Decolonizing my early childhood years and drawing on the work of scholars from the African diaspora birthed anti-racism in ECE. What about you, Flóra? Why anti-racism in ECE?

Flóra: Listening to my grandmothers' stories of the Holocaust, as a child, set me on a path to understand how we can create early childhood environments that will prevent children from growing up to be fascists, racists, misogynists, and so on. Moving to the United States at age 14, it became evidently clear that anti-Black racism in the U.S. is a pervasive social issue. I asked myself, as a white, Jewish, immigrant woman, what is my role in dismantling racism? As someone passionate about child development and early childhood issues, anti-racist early childhood education, and anti-racist parenting of young children, were the answers.

OVERVIEW OF ANTI-RACIST EARLY CHILDHOOD POLICIES

Minoff et al. (2020) define anti-racist early childhood policy as one that is "designed explicitly to redress past injustices, meet the needs of children and families of color, support the whole family, and serve all children and families" (p. 7). In a similar vein, but with a more explicit focus on Black infants and families, via a tripartite procedural framework—i.e., the three pillars of preservation, promotion, and protection—Iruka et al. (2021) examine how extant early years policies may align with expansive anti-racist outcomes in the areas of health, housing, and employment resources, to name a few. Moreover, the framework specifies how to address the limitations of current policies regarding the promotion of positive racial identities for Black children.

Anti-racist early years policymaking—at the state and federal level—consolidates institutional operations, with the express goal of fostering systemic change in ECE. More importantly, policies at both preschools and child care centers carry equivalent critical weight in any wide-ranging reimagining of anti-racism in the early years. Research in a Canadian context sheds light on the impetus for recurrent public dialogues on national programming intended to develop and implement comprehensive anti-racist early years policies.

Notably, in their study on Canadian children's racial awareness and early years educators' approaches to addressing race and racism, Berman and colleagues (2017) found that while many child care centers adopted anti-racist policies, the effectiveness of such guidelines was often hindered by educators' color-blind attitudes, which influenced how they perceived racial incidents and their implications for young children. At a center-based level, for anti-racist policies to aspire to such uncompromising goals as identifying racism, protecting racialized children and families, and creating a space of belonging and safety, North American educators need to collectively receive mandatory and ongoing training in anti-racist pedagogy.

DEVELOPING AN ANTI-RACIST EARLY CHILDHOOD POLICY: ESSENTIAL ELEMENTS OF AUTHORSHIP

When creating anti-racist policies, educators and administrators must proceed with a renewed emphasis on anti-racist guiding principles. We argue that the voices and views of racialized and subjugated peoples are central to policymaking, especially with the intent to combat racism and safeguard children's well-being. If the operator of a child care center does not originate from a racialized background or does not have recourse to the requisite training, then it is incumbent on that individual to acquire training from anti-racist experts in the field to assist with conceptualizing, drafting, and preparing anti-racist guidelines.

Content: What Is Your Institutional Mission and Vision?

In addition to defining key terms such as *race, racism, anti-racism,* and *intersectionality,* anti-racist policies must support a well-defined pedagogical vision for child care centers and preschools. Contributing policymakers should consider what an anti-racist vision "looks like" for their organization and how best practices can be operationalized. For example, an anti-racist vision can serve as the conceptual framework for developing attendant anti-racist quality rating scales/systems for early years programs. In crafting an anti-racist mission statement, organizations must develop specific goals pertinent to various stakeholders, including children, parents, faculty and/or staff members, and the local community.

The process of identifying these goals involves an examination of the distinguishing features of anti-racist pedagogy—such as the learning outcomes associated with race and unequal power relationships—and adheres to guidelines for using an analysis of these features to co-create germane educational solutions. For example, the lack of representation on staff and unredressed salaries for Black and racialized women are two ways in which white privilege and power permeate early learning spaces. An anti-racist preschool strategic plan may commit to recruiting and retaining Black and racialized staff, providing them with an equitable wage and opportunities for advancement.

Context: Educator Training and Reporting Racial Incidents

Racial incidents continue to occur at child care centers across Canada and the United States, with Black children often unduly disciplined and harmed. Consequently, anti-racist policies for early childhood classrooms urge anti-racist training for educators and administrators in case of racial incidents implicating a child, a parent, a care provider, and/or an educator. Parents of the affected children should be notified immediately after the incident, with follow-up meetings coordinated by primary administrators and attended by educators. Meetings need to be conducted in a way that parents of children who commit racist offenses are reappraised of the center's zero- tolerance policy regarding racism and provided with resources about anti-racist parenting strategies (for repeated offenses, termination of the family's contract should be implemented). Meetings need to also address the child or children who were harmed, and reparation and healing strategies should be discussed to minimize further harm and trauma.

Training in anti-racism at pre- and inservice child care posts should be a prerequisite in early years programs. To be able to identify and report racial incidents, early childhood educators benefit from meaningful administrative support. Anti-racist policymaking directs staff to receive open-ended professional development instruction in anti-racist pedagogy and participate in communities of practice to share their growth. The missions of anti-racist early years organizations lend themselves to an initiative-taking approach whereby administrative processes ensure that potential employees share a corresponding commitment to anti-racism. Qualifying interviews, for example, might include administrative discussions about a center's anti-racist policy, or requests for applicants to share a practical summation of their own anti-racist practices.

Benefits of Anti-Racist Early Years Policies for Children

Anti-racist policies and practices benefit all children, particularly young, racialized children. In the context of anti-racist policies, racialized children will develop racial pride and positive racial identities. Anti-racist policies can support educators in providing curricular and classroom materials that affirm BIPOC children's identities in classroom materials and the curricula. Representation is a cornerstone of developing a positive racial identity, especially for children of color. As the adage goes, "You can't be what you can't see." However, representation is not enough. As one study reflects (Holmes et al., 2017), some teachers acknowledge that representation is not a substitute for explicitly teaching about race. Children deserve the time and space to discuss race and racism (Holmes et al., 2017). Anti-racist policies will allow children to have the time and space in early childhood settings to have their voices heard about race and racism. For young Black, Indigenous, and racialized children, it is especially important to have the freedom to express their thoughts, perspectives, identities, and experiences around their racialized experiences. Anti-racist policies can encourage early childhood educators to support racialized children in countering internalized oppression via conversations, book readings, films, and other methods, including the arts and collaboration with community members. Anti-racist policies can ensure that BIPOC children learn to honor their own and others' full humanity, including those of other BIPOC children.

Anti-racist early childhood policies can also benefit white children. Young white children will learn to identify their own racial privilege and biases, and counter this in themselves and in white peers. Importantly, young white children will recognize how to use their privilege for social change and will learn examples about how to serve as allies and accomplices to racialized children and families in the fight for racial justice. In the absence of anti-racist policies and practices, we risk white children developing internalized racial superiority and reproducing white supremacy. Thus, anti-racist policies and practices in early childhood are not only a form of intervention to reduce harm for BIPOC children, but also support white children's anti-racist consciousness.

For both BIPOC and white children, anti-racist early childhood policies and practices hold promise in teaching children about activism and actions against racial injustice. Even young children need opportunities to move beyond reflecting on their own beliefs and identities, and to move toward actions and concrete steps in creating social justice (e.g., Kessler & Swadener, 2020). Young children have the capacity to engage in individual or collective action to fight oppression, especially if adults provide support for this (Heberle et al., in press).

For Educators

Anti-racist policies and practices hold great promise for educators. Anti-racist policies will support educators to reflect on their own biases about families who are racially different from themselves. Self-reflection is a critical component to improving teaching practices in general, and this is certainly the case for beliefs as deep-seated as those held about race (Lin et al., 2008). Anti-racist policies support educators in implementing anti-racist practices, practices that educators may be hesitant to implement for fear of backlash from administrators and from some families. If educators have anti-racist policies on the books, they may feel a great sense of support and protection when implementing practices that may be controversial in the current sociopolitical climate in which critical race theory is under attack. Anti-racist policies may encourage teachers to prioritize family and community engagement, so that BIPOC families and community members can share and control their own narratives when communicating about race and racism.

For the Early Years Field

Anti-racist early childhood policies hold a tremendous potential to transform the early years field and to move the field from anti-bias to anti-racism (see Escayg, 2018). Anti-bias education is more focused on individual biases and prejudices, whereas anti-racist education is more focused on addressing systemic and racial inequities baked into the early years systems such as white privilege, white power, white supremacy, and institutional racism (Escayg, 2018). Incorporating anti-racism into early childhood education will allow educators to make educational experiences more relevant to racialized children and families by incorporating their lived realities and perspectives into the curriculum (Escayg, 2018). However, intersectionality will need to be addressed as part of anti-racist policies and practices (Escayg, 2018). Boys of color, not just boys or just children of color, are disproportionately impacted by racial disparities in preschool discipline (Shivers et al., 2021). Addressing intersectionality within anti-racist early childhood frameworks will allow the field to counter the disproportionate pushing of young boys and girls of color into the cradle-to-prison-pipeline or nexus. Anti-racism will allow the field to aspire to the National Association for the Education of Young Children's (NAEYC) goal to provide "all children the right to equitable learning opportunities that help them achieve their full potential as engaged learners and valued members of society."

In conclusion, anti-racist early childhood policies represent one critical step toward transforming traditional practices in the field, many of which derive from social, cultural, and economic racialized power. To ensure equitable practice, to ensure that Black children and racialized children thrive in the fullness and essence of their respective identities, we need institutional interventions at all levels. Policies provide promise, a hope for substantive change; more importantly, however, policies must protect. The children—our children—are waiting.

REFERENCES

Berman, R., Daniel, B. J., Butler, A., MacNevin, M., & Royer, N. (2017). Nothing, or almost nothing, to report: Early childhood educators and discursive constructions of colorblindness. *International Critical Childhood Policy Studies Journal, 6*(1), 52–65.

Escayg, K-A. (2018). The missing links: Enhancing anti-bias education with anti-racist education. *Journal of Curriculum, Teaching, Learning and Leadership in Education, 3*(1), 15–20.

Escayg, K-A. (2019). Who's got the power? *International Journal of Child Care and Education Policy, 13*(1), 1–18.

Heberle, A., Faragó, F., & Hoch, N. (in press). Critical consciousness in early to middle childhood. In L. Rapa & E. Godfrey (Eds.), *Critical consciousness.* Cambridge University Press.

Holmes, K. A., Garcia, J., & Adair, J. K. (2017). Who said we're too young to talk about race? First graders and their teacher investigate racial justice through counter-stories. In N. Yelland & D. F. Bentley (Eds.), *Found in translation* (pp. 129–147). Routledge.

Iruka, I. U., Harper, K., Lloyd, C. M., Boddicker-Young, P., De Marco, A., & Blanding, J. (2021*). Anti-racist policymaking to protect, promote, and preserve Black families and babies.* Frank Porter Graham Child Development Institute.

Kessler, S. A., & Swadener, B. B. (Eds.). (2020). *Educating for social justice in early childhood.* Routledge.

Lin, M., Lake, V. E., & Rice, D. (2008). Teaching anti-bias curriculum in teacher education programs. *Teacher Education Quarterly, 35*(2), 187–200.

Minoff, E, Citrin, A., Martínez, V., & Martin, M. (2020). *What we owe young children.* Center for the Study of Social Policy.

Shivers, E. M., Faragó, F., & Gal-Szabo, D. (2021). The role of infant and early childhood mental health consultation in reducing racial and gender relational and discipline disparities between Black and white preschoolers. *Psychology in the Schools.* https://doi.org/10.1002/pits.22573

Short- and Long-Term Policy Solutions Are Necessary to Address Inequities in Access and Affordability in the Early Years

Chrishana M. Lloyd and Julianna Carlson

To improve the accessibility and affordability of early child care and education (ECE) in the United States, we must first understand how we got to a place where ECE is in short supply and prohibitively expensive for most families with young children. We tell this story by exploring forces, both historical and contemporary, that have shaped the early years system that currently exists in our country. As noted by our colleagues in the book's opening section, this system is fragmented, where access to high-quality, affordable child care is a challenge for many, but is also exponentially more difficult for some. We shed light on this challenge, as well as why caring for and educating the youngest people in our society is so undervalued, despite its critical importance to our country's success. We also highlight the ways these issues affect the early years workforce, as well as families and children, and end with suggestions for policies to address these wrongdoings.

HISTORY OF RACISM, SEXISM, CAPITALISM, AND EARLY CARE AND EDUCATION

The ECE story is an important one. The challenges in the system affect both professionals and families with young children in the United States. Importantly, these practices and policies occur at multiple levels—structural, institutional, and individual. For example, in their chapter calling for anti-racist policies in child care and preschools, Kerry-Ann Escayg and Flóra Faragó highlight how racist practices and policies can be found in national, state, and local policies (structural level), in organizations such

47

as child care settings and preschool classrooms (institutional level), and by ECE professionals via parent, child, or professional-to-professional interactions and exchanges (individual level).

These multiple and tiered manifestations of racism in ECE (along with colonialist and sexist practices and policies) also serve as a foundation on which capitalism in the United States rests. For instance, at its inception, our country was designed to enrich the lives of a select group of individuals—white European men and their white families. As such, the first practices and policies to promote this goal included the theft of land from Native American people; the kidnapping, enslavement, and selling of Black people; the rape and forced impregnation of Black women; and the relegation of white women to domesticity.

These activities were core to generating profit for white men in what would eventually become the United States. Capitalism also requires work and reproduction to ensure an ongoing pool of labor and a productive society. As such, child care became a necessary part of the economic infrastructure of the country, and families with young children had difficulty participating in work without it. As a result, ECE became—and still is—a necessary component of the economic infrastructure of the country.

A capitalist society also results in hierarchies. Certain groups and professions must be at the bottom for those at the top to profit. In the United States minoritized people, including Native, Black, Hispanic, and select groups of Asian Americans, are the least valued and most disempowered. By design, these individuals tend to be employed in lower-wage jobs, resulting in them being at the bottom of the economic ladder in the United States.

Women and people working in caretaking professions like ECE (a primarily female-dominated field with significant numbers of minoritized and women of color) are also devalued socially and economically. Throughout American history, Black women have been forced into domestic labor, including child care. This shoehorning occurred during the enslavement of Black people in the United States and has continued for centuries. Layered onto these issues is the belief by many in the country that child care is a private issue, one in which the public should have no role in supporting. As a result, the child care profession in the United States has been marginalized within ECE's fragmented system—associated with Black women, perceived to require minimal skill, and thought to be undeserving of respect or adequate compensation (Lloyd et al., 2022).

These overwhelmingly negative, prevalent, and longstanding ideologies have served to maintain and often perpetuate inequity for ECE workers and the families and young children who need care and education. For example, the Fair Labor and Standards Act of 1938, which introduced guaranteed wages and standard hours for American workers, explicitly excluded domestic (i.e., child care and home-based) workers. Even well-intentioned policies may have unintended consequences that maintain or entrench racism and inequity. For instance, a recent federal program designed to help small businesses during the COVID-19 pandemic has been implemented in ways that disadvantage child care businesses operated by women of color (LaRocca, 2020).

ONGOING INEQUITIES IN TODAY'S FRAGMENTED SYSTEM

To reiterate what was laid out in Section I of this book, our current ECE system is fragmented. It is funded through a complex combination of monies (private, state, and federal) and delivered in a variety of settings (home-, community-, and school-based). This structure as well as the funding mechanisms present many challenges. For instance, child care settings are not financed similarly or equitably, which has led to differential compensation and professional development supports for the ECE workforce, as well as variation in access and costs for families with young children. Often these differences are racialized. The number of ECE professionals who are minoritized and/or of color is higher in settings like unregulated home-based child care, for example (Whitebook et al., 2018).

These home-based professionals tend not to be a part of the formal system and are also more likely than other provider types (e.g., center- or school-based) to have limited access to fiscal resources and professional development supports. In addition, home-based child care professionals are more likely to serve higher numbers of families with children who are demographically and geographically similar to them, which means the families and children who they work with also tend to be minoritized, of color, and/or have less access to fiscal and other resources (Lloyd et al., 2019). Conversely, ECE professionals who are white tend to work in settings with higher levels of compensation, such as center- and school-based programs; serve families who are more affluent and/or economically advantaged; and are employed in settings that have more access to resources and professional development (Staub-Johnson, 2018). Despite these realities, as Ashley May's powerful essay shows (Chapter 4, this volume), it should never be forgotten that home-based professionals possess great cultural wealth.

RACISM IN U.S. SYSTEMS DEEPENS CHALLENGES FOR FAMILIES WITH YOUNG CHILDREN

When we turn our gaze to families, the hierarchies mentioned above are also present. Access to child care means access to employment, and in turn to higher earnings, economic stability, and better physical and mental health for families with young children. Unfortunately, systemic barriers limit access to ECE for certain families, particularly those who are minoritized and/or of color. For instance, we know that the cost for high-quality child care is prohibitively expensive for many Black families. We also know that Black families are less likely than families of any other race to have child care centers in their neighborhoods, making affordability and access to child care a challenge. This reinforces and exacerbates already existing issues that stem from systemic racism, including limiting the ability of adults in families to work.

POLICY RECOMMENDATIONS

Making ECE affordable, accessible, and equitable requires an understanding and changing of the structures and systems that have kept it unaffordable, inaccessible, and inequitable. To date, most attempts to improve the dimensions of the ECE system that promote inequity have had a narrow focus—programs or policies that provide short-term fixes instead of aiming to transform the overarching systems that maintain inequities.

The COVID-19 pandemic has exposed and amplified the challenges of the ECE system, bringing wide attention to issues like racial inequalities in workforce compensation and child care deserts. At the same time, the pandemic has also created a unique opportunity to reimagine the system. With increased public awareness about the value of child care and its importance to the country's economic recovery, there is a critical window of opportunity to advocate for large-scale change through policy solutions that are centered in justice. In the spirit of promoting racial and gender justice in ECE, and building on Jacqueline Jones's recommendations in Chapter 3, we suggest the following five strategies to build a sustainable and more equitable system for caring for and educating young children.

1. SHIFT THE NARRATIVE THAT EQUITABLE PRACTICES RELATED TO ACCESSIBILITY AND AFFORDABILITY IN ECE ONLY BENEFIT A SELECT FEW

The history of our country tells us that colonialist, racist, sexist, oppressive, and discriminatory practices exist on multiple levels of society (structural, institutional, and individual). We also know that people will engage in these damaging practices both consciously and subconsciously, and that these behaviors cause direct harm to the intended individuals, often disadvantaging those who are inflicting harm, too (McGhee, 2021). In the ECE field, this type of irrational behavior halts progress for minoritized people,

people of color, and women—and like in society more generally, it also results in harm to everyone.

Shining a truthful and critical eye on the history of our country and highlighting the negative ways minoritized people, people of color, and women have been (and continue to be) disadvantaged is a first step toward developing an honest foundation on which ECE policies can be designed and implemented to right historic wrongs related to child care access and affordability. This type of strategy will require significant coalition-building and political maneuvering.

It will also require the dismantling of false narratives and incorrect equivalents, such as the idea that support for minoritized and people of color is anti-white. White people in particular—both men and women—will be key to successful implementation of this strategy. The power and access to resources that has been bestowed upon white people in the United States is substantial. We also know that despite laudable and sustained efforts over centuries, minoritized people and people of color have yet to be successful in ameliorating these issues on their own. We call on white people and others in positions of power to recognize the struggle, raise their voices, and actively take on this issue for the betterment of the early child care and education field and society at large.

2.   INCREASE PUBLIC INVESTMENT IN ECE

Early child care and education is critical to the infrastructure of our country. As such, we believe that ECE should be considered a public good. Expanding government support and allocating robust funding to ECE has the potential to result in greater U.S. economic growth and a stronger country. High-quality ECE facilitates the development of more productive citizens and outcomes such as strengthened social skills, better school outcomes, and increased lifetime earnings, which are beneficial for society and the public at large.

3.   EASE THE CHILD CARE COST BURDEN FOR FAMILIES

Along with increased public investment, we call for attention to equity in direct child care costs for families. Policies currently used to curb ECE costs include strategies like subsidies, child care tax credits, and sliding scales to help make child care more affordable. Even with these strategies, many families are still struggling. We recommend ECE policy solutions that consider issues like the cost of living and housing, family debt (e.g., student loans, mortgages), and home ownership. Consideration and weighting of factors like these can result in more affordable ECE costs that take into account the lack of a historically level playing field for certain families.

4. ENSURE THAT THE ECE WORKFORCE IS COMPENSATED AT RATES THAT ALLOW THEM TO CARE FOR THEMSELVES AND THEIR FAMILIES

ECE professionals are some of the lowest-paid workers in the country, with many accessing public benefits to stay afloat. Like parents, we need those serving our nation's children to have the resources they need to be well prepared to care for our youngest and greatest national resource. Making child care a public rather than private responsibility, increasing compensation for ECE professionals, and equalizing compensation for those who have experienced or been impacted by issues like colonialism and racism is the morally right thing to do for ECE professionals, families, young children, and the country as a whole.

5. IMPLEMENT NATIONWIDE PARENTAL LEAVE POLICIES

The transition to parenthood is challenging, and children are time-consuming and costly. We want to emphasize Jacqueline Jones's mention of universal parental leave as a good first start to better supporting families until movement can be made on the more expensive, and arguably more challenging to implement, recommendations made above. Given the dearth of high-quality, affordable ECE options for families and the broad support from large swaths of U.S. citizens that parental leave policies have, we think universal parental leave is an important stopgap measure until steps can be taken to improve the access and affordability of ECE for families.

We recognize that major shifts will be needed in public sentiment and resource allocation to realize the recommendations we have put forth. Though challenging, we stand by the importance of these recommendations and call for others to align with us to advance an ECE system that benefits *all* of our nation's ECE workers, families, and children.

REFERENCES

LaRocca, A. (2020). *Home Grown technical assistance program for the Paycheck Protection Program.* Home Grown. https://homegrownchildcare.org/wp-content/uploads/2020/12/Home-Grown-PPP-Project-Outcomes-Report_Luminary_Septembr-2020.pdf

Lloyd, C. M., Carlson, J., Barnett, H., Shaw, S., & Logan, D. (2022). *Mary Pauper: A historical exploration of early care and education compensation, policy, and solutions*. Child Trends.

Lloyd, C. M., Kane, M., Seok, D., & Vega, C. (2019). *Examining the feasibility of using home visiting models to support home-based child care providers*. Child Trends.

McGhee, H. C. (2021). *The sum of us*. One World.

Staub-Johnson, C. (2018). *Equity starts early*. Center for Law and Social Policy.

Whitebook, M., McLean, C., Austin, L. J. E., & Edwards, B. (2018). *Early childhood workforce index—2018*. Center for the Study of Child Care Employment.

Part III

FELT IN/EQUITIES IN THE EARLY YEARS

Infant/Toddler Care and Education

In an already marginalized early years sector in the United States, infant/ toddler programs, teachers, and roles are among the most misunderstood and undercompensated. Persistent views of people and programs serving children birth to 3 include persistent notions of babysitting that ignore how critical these years are to a child's development, well-being, and relationships. Longtime practitioners, professional development specialists, and researchers in these earliest ages frame issues, share powerful stories, and recommend policies that place this area of care and learning in the foreground in important ways. Barbara Milner draws on 30 years of experience supporting young children and their families to frame the state of the field, and Emmanuelle Fincham reflects on earning her PhD while remaining a toddler teacher and brings feminist and anti-racist reflections on inequities in the field to the fore. The section concludes with recommendations from Emily Sharrock and Annie Schaeffing for policy related to professional recognition, equitable compensation, and better understanding of the significance of those who work with the youngest children.

CHAPTER 7

Felt In/equities

The Status of Infant/Toddler Care

Barbara Milner

Caring for young children in groups has been a part of the culture in the United States for a considerable time, but the number of families needing out-of-home care for their very young children has increased dramatically. When I started my career in the field of early childhood care and education over 30 years ago, the number of child care programs serving the birth to 3 age group was significantly lower than today. There are many reports highlighting the changes in society that impact the number of infants and toddlers in group care. Along with the increased demand, a growing body of research over the past several decades has established the importance of high-quality infant/toddler care to children's positive development. However, it is also widely recognized that a troubling percentage of very young children in the United States are in child care settings that are considered to be of minimal or even poor quality and that children from lower-income families are most frequently enrolled in the lowest-quality programs (Loeb et al., 2004).

The COVID-19 pandemic has brought new attention to early childhood care and the increasingly fragile system that many experts would say has been in crisis for years. These complex issues are not new (as discussed in Part 1) or solely caused by the pandemic, but have called attention to how critical child care is for the U.S. economy. The importance of understanding the complexities and inequities regarding child care in the United States is critical, especially if specific challenges facing infant/toddler care and education will be addressed. Concerns regarding the inequities between elementary school and preschool systems in the United States have been voiced and well documented for many years (as discussed by Emmanuelle Fincham in Chapter 8). Another inequity not as widely discussed outside the early childhood field, and not nearly enough within it, is the comparison between preschool and the infant and toddler age groups. Although the "versus" debate is not new, this recent national attention provides an opportunity and platform to explore and better understand the experiences of our youngest children in group care, as well as their teachers' experiences.

The importance of high-quality child care and the increased demand for infant/toddler care in the United States has been identified, but have these needs been addressed in societal support and U.S. policy? Unfortunately, any social changes did not include successful efforts to revolutionize the child care system in the United States, as has happened in most other developed countries. Paid parental leave is an example of policy that impacts infants and allows families the choice to delay returning to work after the addition of a new baby. In his work to highlight how U.S. policies negatively impact babies, Ronald Lally (2013) reported that only three other countries—Liberia, Papua New Guinea, and Swaziland—along with the United States, do not provide nationwide paid parental leave for mothers in any segment of the workforce. In the United States the role of the government in child care is underfunded, limited, and fragmented.

Defining the complex issues facing us is an ongoing challenge confronted by advocates working for critical policy change. My experiences as a parent and as a professional highlight some of the ongoing inequities and complexities faced by families, our workforce, and infants and toddlers. It is relevant to mention that when I first observed in a child care program as a college student, I was not a parent myself. Not only was I unsure of what quality infant/toddler care looked like, I did not realize the emotions of child care issues.

CARE VERSUS EDUCATION IN INFANT/TODDLER SETTINGS

When I was hired in 1983 for my first full-time job teaching 2–3-year-olds, my daughter was an infant. Because the program I worked for did not accept children who were not potty-trained, I found care for my daughter in a family child care home. I was told when I was hired that this child care center focused on education, so this child care center's owner decided that having infants and young toddlers would take away from the goal of educating young children. Although this explanation didn't feel fair to me as a parent of an infant who needed child care, I did not understand then the complexity or implications of the situation.

This was my first experience regarding an ongoing debate of care versus education and access to quality child care for infants and toddlers. In my early career and as a parent, I quickly recognized that the needs of very young children were not being served well in many group care settings. This awareness started with just a feeling that was difficult to articulate. I did not know what I did not know. Yet we now know considerably more about what is best for young children by what research tells us, and we still face wide gaps between what we know and what is happening in the care of our youngest children.

Workforce issues in infant/toddler care are one of the wide gaps where the latest research is not influencing our systems. As a young parent who found family child care (nonrelative care provided in someone else's home) as the only affordable option for my infant daughter, I was faced with frequent changes (provider needing extended time off, closing their business, or unreliable care) that caused stress and concern for my child's experiences in group care.

The limited options and stability of care available continue to impact families. The turnover rate of early childhood teachers is often mentioned in reports regarding child care issues, often citing low pay and lack of benefits as primary reasons. It is unfortunate that in the United States, concerns regarding low pay are a familiar topic about teachers for children in all age groups, from birth through high school. Retention of infant/toddler teachers has many implications for young children, caregivers, and programs, but especially infants and toddlers for whom change in caregivers is far from ideal. The changes in caregivers and the factors affecting retention are not simplistic or easily explained, especially to the larger public. There are so many issues facing the infant/toddler care and education workforce.

PROFESSIONAL RECOGNITION AND REGULATION IN THE INFANT/TODDLER SECTOR

My colleague Emmanuelle Fincham will discuss the societal assumptions and values often associated with infant/toddler care teachers in the following chapter. The importance of terminology when describing the challenges can often become a barrier. Even the term *teacher* can feel to some individuals as absent of an equally important component of the job, which is the caregiving role, begging the question of how seldom *teacher* is used for this work. Some advocates prefer the name "care teacher" to highlight the importance of both the facilitation of care and learning this role includes. This is just one example of the nuances to describe this important work with infants and toddlers.

To better understand the unique workforce challenges for infant/toddler care, we must also discuss the impact of child care regulations. In the United States, where investments in a child care system have been avoided, the absence of a federal child care agenda leaves mandatory standards to be dictated by the regulatory system in state, county, and city governments, primarily by health and human services agencies. This inconsistency between our states causes confusion and contributes to the struggle facing advocates who are trying to elevate the importance of child care and prioritize the rights of our youngest.

Another component of regulations that has implications for our workforce is the requirements for hiring. Regulations usually include the educational requirements and prior experience recommendations for positions in a child care program. These legal requirements can become one of the gaps we need to address. In states that are considered "low licensing states," such as Arizona, where I live, these regulations often have very minimum qualifications for teachers and directors. In Arizona, a high school diploma or GED, background check, and 6 months of child care experience are required before a person can be hired as a teacher in a child care program. After a mandatory brief orientation, a person then has a year to obtain the required 18 hours of annual professional development training.

This translates into a message that care teachers do not require prior specialized education and preparation for their role in classrooms. With just a high school education or GED, no felony charges in your background, and a small amount of experience, you can be alone in a classroom with young children, responsible for their care and learning needs. Comparatively, in Arizona, the requirements that our state mandates by law for another profession, a nail technician (licensed to provide manicures and pedicures), include job training and skill assessment prior to employment. The Arizona State Board of Cosmetology requires individuals seeking licensure to receive up to 600 *hours* of training from an approved cosmetology school and be able to pass a test that proves that you have the skills and knowledge to practice in the field before a nail technician can perform duties or touch anyone's cuticles.

This comparison does not mean to imply that the mandatory preparation for a licensed nail technician is too stringent, but is meant to highlight the value being communicated to society regarding the role of care teachers and to argue strongly that this is another example of ignoring the human rights of infants and toddlers. Are the rights of infants and toddlers to be cared for and educated by a well-prepared workforce as important as the health and safety of our finger- and toenails? The implications in the field for hiring with these low requirements are an underprepared, undervalued, and underresourced workforce.

Research has shown us the importance of brain development in the first 3 years and its impact on future learning, yet we are not preparing our workforce adequately for their important roles in our youngest children's lives. Even when individuals seek academic achievement in preparation for a career with very young children, we have critical gaps to address. Most of my academic studies of early childhood education had primarily focused on the preschool years. When studying child development theories, more time was focused on the preschool years and examples given were often of one child, not how this developmental stage would look and feel with a group of young children the same age together. My academic journey did not include best practices for caring for young children in groups, the unique needs of infants and toddlers, or the policies of other countries regarding family options and care of babies and young children. When seeking specialized professional development regarding infants and toddlers, I often needed to travel out of state.

Regulations also can impede the building of relationships between care teachers and children. Attachment theory and research continue to stress the critical importance of early attachments. The quality of the relationship between the infant and teacher has been reported to be the most important factor for their development (Administration for Children & Families, 2018). Child care programs must ensure that each young child has a chance to have sustained experiences with a care teacher assigned to be their primary or special teacher and to develop a secure attachment. It takes time for an adult to become familiar to a child, especially infants. Close reciprocal relationships do not happen overnight. Experts recommend the relationship between child and care teacher to be ongoing, ideally from the infancy period to 36 months. But the best practice of continuity of care is impeded by large group sizes, high adult-to-child ratios, and additional regulations that enforce children moving to different classrooms based on their birthdates, classifying rooms as 1-year old, 2-year-old, and so forth. Also, the high turnover of practitioners is a factor. We are not supporting best practices to be implemented and sustained.

There have been many examples of efforts across our country to address these gaps and provide support for quality improvement within our current system. Examples include states making changes in their regulatory laws and implementing a quality rating system. However, when quality improvement efforts do not support program leadership and care teachers to understand both the "why" for the best practices being recommended and the "how" to implement them, these efforts will continue to largely fall on the shoulders of our care teachers. Between lack of care teacher preparation, insufficient specialized professional development, and daily program operations that follow narrow regulations that do not include policies for what is best for infants and toddlers, we are creating work environments that have professional expectations without professional conditions.

Infants and toddlers have care and learning needs that are distinct from preschool children. Having a skilled, knowledgeable, well-prepared, and supported workforce that understands the unique needs of very young children is essential for ensuring that these children receive the care and delicate balance of stimulation and consistent, predictable routines they need to thrive. The need for society and all members of our field to understand the differences in infant and toddler group care and to take the numerous findings into consideration is critical to develop a new approach and commitment to ensure that infants and toddlers have the beginning they deserve.

REFERENCES

Administration for Children & Families, Child Care State Capacity Building Center. (2018). *Respectful and responsive relationships are key to supporting optimal infant and toddler development.* https://childcareta.acf.hhs.gov/resource/respectful-and-responsive-relationships-are-key-supporting-optimal-infant-and-toddler

Lally, R. J. (2013) *For our babies.* Teachers College Press and WestEd.

Loeb, S., Fuller, B., Kagan, S. L., & Carrol, B. (2004). *Child care in poor communities.* Society for Research in Child Development, Inc.

CHAPTER 8

Felt In/equities

The Status of Infant/Toddler Teachers

Emmanuelle N. Fincham

I vividly remember watching a talk show years ago where a host complained about having to attend their toddler's nursery school back-to-school night, commenting, "What are they gonna tell us about, Play-Doh?" This comment garnered the laughter it was meant to, and it let me know, as a teacher of young children, that most people are unlikely to have respect for the work I do. As an infant/toddler teacher for the last 15 years, I have too often been faced with comments relating my work to "babysitting," rife with assumptions that this is an unskilled, nonintellectual role. Yet, in reality, many "babysitters" are quite skilled home-based educators and caregivers, often uniquely qualified to sustain cultural-linguistic family practices.

These disparaging perspectives are rooted deeply in assumptions regarding infants and toddlers. Societal assumptions and policies around caring for young children stem from theories and ideas of the past, many of which sustain ideas of the infant and young child as incapable, unaware, and in need of constant care, supervision, and guidance. Given this construction as highly "needy" beings, it is no surprise that the teaching of infants and toddlers is seen primarily as basic caregiving and, as such, "unskilled" work for women, who are "naturally" able to care for young children. Female teachers are estimated to make up the vast majority of the early childhood field. Among these, women of color are disproportionately employed in low-wage child care positions (McLean et al., 2021). These statistics reflect dominant assumptions that women—primarily women who are nonwhite and non-middle/upper class—are best suited for caring for young children and that they will do it for little pay.

Drawing on stories from my personal experience as an infant/toddler teacher and teacher educator, I will further accentuate these issues. Sharing my stories, I must acknowledge and forefront that my privilege as a white educator has unquestioningly granted me access to spaces that exclude many and allows me to be seen differently by a societal gaze that assumes much about women in low-wage care work. While my stories and experiences are likely relatable, I do not claim to speak for the field or to understand the experiences of other infant/toddler teachers with whom I stand in solidarity. There is great variability in funding, curriculum, employment, and regulation across infant and toddler care and education settings in the United States; nevertheless, the issues I attend to here reverberate in numerous ways throughout the field.

IT'S WOMEN'S WORK AND YOU'RE A WOMAN, SO . . .

While completing my early childhood certification, I was working as a visiting teaching artist in a city-funded child care center in New York City. I loved this school. I adored those kids. I respected and learned so much from all the teachers I worked with there, all of whom were women of color. I talked to the director about the prospect of a teaching position with the toddlers, the age group that interested me the most. She was ecstatic that I was making the shift to classroom teacher but was very upfront with me about the salary she could offer, informing me that "someone of my qualification could get a much better job." I did the math and realized that this salary would be a drop in my current income that came from various part-time jobs. And even though I lived in a "cheap" (by New York City standards) apartment, I was concerned that I wouldn't be able to cover my rent and other expenses (including soon-to-begin student loan payments) on the salary she could offer.

Putting this experience into context, my graduate school colleagues were getting teaching jobs in public elementary schools for at least twice the salary of teachers at the small city-funded early childhood center. Additionally, the early childhood center teachers were working a full 12-month contract, with a longer day on-site than the typical elementary school schedule. For new early childhood teachers, graduating with the same qualifications and same certifications, there are great disparities in teachers' salaries across the early childhood age range, which in New York and many other states covers infants through 2nd grade. Early childhood teachers are expected to attain higher education in order to gain certification, but most often the cost of schooling and the process of certification do not correspond with the low-wage positions available to those who want to teach infants and toddlers.

When I first decided to pursue a degree and certification in early childhood, I did a lot of work (as most teachers do) to convince myself that I was not "in it for the money." The intrinsic value and my "calling" to work with very young children were supposed to be enough, or at least those were the messages I received my whole life. Teachers (of any age) have been socially, historically, and discursively produced to martyr themselves, giving of their time and worth for the good of the children. This mirrors the positioning of women in the United States as inferior to men, archaic notions that still hold strong today as we continue to see the discrimination of women across professions.

Madeleine Grumet (1988) called attention to how teaching is discursively constructed as "women's work," where expectations of womanly intuition often silence intellect. This assumption is especially granted to those who teach very young children. Since the care and education of very young children are perceived as something that comes "naturally" to women and was expected to be addressed in the home, expectations for infant and toddler teachers rarely stretch beyond what many see as instinctive care and nurturing practices. This perspective on the work of women who care for and educate our youngest children leads to a greatly diminished status for teachers who bring immeasurable competencies to their practice. Yet, their work remains unvalued and unrecognized, rendering them invisible in the field of education.

BUT I WANT TO TEACH IN A "REAL" SCHOOL

In my first years of teaching, I remember how turned off I was when parents referred to our center as "day care." As an "educated" teacher who chose to work with infants, I was adamant that our center was just as worthy to be called a "school" as any other. It hit even harder when I overheard a conversation between a parent and one of my student teachers. The parent asked her if she liked working in the infant classroom and if she wanted to keep working with infants. Without a second's hesitation, the student teacher replied, "No, I think I want to work in a real school." I'm pretty sure my heart stopped for a moment as I processed this comment from across the room. This was a student I had worked alongside with and mentored for an entire semester. Yet, on this, one of her last days in my classroom, I was struck with the realization that she may still have no understanding of the work I did as a teacher.

The care versus education debate has hindered progress in the field of early childhood for far too long. The constructed binary of care/education has led to mutually exclusive understandings of the terms that are, in reality, completely embedded in each other and simultaneously occurring in the work of infant-toddler teachers. "Care" is held up as the basis of the work, leading to assumptions that anyone with basic knowledge and instincts can take care of infants and young children. On the other side of the coin, efforts to professionalize the work of infant/toddler teachers have sought to position "education" above care, striving for the same status as those whose primary role is to "educate" older children. As this story of my student teacher's comment illustrates, this predicament is surprisingly yet especially experienced in teacher education programs that are preparing teachers to work with children from birth through age 8.

Even within the field of early childhood, infants and toddlers seem to be positioned in a space of "pre-childhood," as their experiences in classrooms are hardly represented in the literature compared to the presumed "more important" schooling experiences of older children. This is reflected in teacher education programs that focus on preparing teachers for preschool and primary classrooms, with little more than basic knowledge of infants and toddlers. These practices perpetuate assumptions around teaching infants and toddlers that stem from competing discourses of professionalism and care, where teaching jobs with older children continue to be positioned as more "professional."

INCREASING THE VISIBILITY AND STATUS OF INFANTS, TODDLERS, AND THEIR TEACHERS

So, how do we address these issues? How can we, those of us engaging daily with infants and toddlers, be heard? What can we do to increase representation of the work we do and the innumerable capabilities of infants and toddlers and possibilities for constructing curriculum and pedagogy with our youngest children? To answer these questions, we must pursue a multitiered approach that involves changes in practice, the preparation of teachers, research, and policy. Drawing on my experiences, I put forth two broad recommendations for teachers, researchers, teacher educators, and advocates to consider.

First and foremost, we must work across the field to better understand the complexity of infants and toddlers, which for too long has been masked by the simplicity of developmental knowledge based on stage theories. To do so, we must engage and value new research that develops from the classroom level, including qualitative work that prioritizes the roles and knowledges of those working with infants and toddlers on a daily basis. This work will highlight caring practices and perspectives that also refuse to assume young children's incapability of understanding the world in more complex ways. Connecting classroom-based research with contemporary brain research, which illustrates how infants and toddlers are much more competent and insightful than previously assumed, will usher in a new way of being with and learning about children from birth. At the same time, we will be opening spaces for understandings that involve more culturally responsive and culturally sustaining ways of teaching and caring for infants and toddlers.

Second, as my colleagues in this section emphasize, is the need to professionalize care work as a part of education rather than something separate. This is double-edged, as the push must come from policy that both raises the expectations for infant/toddler teachers and also supports higher salaries for teachers in the field. Another piece of this process must happen in early childhood teacher education programs that have neglected the study of infants and toddlers. There needs to be increased representation and field experiences with infants and toddlers in teacher education programs in order to shift the discourses that perpetuate the low status of infant/toddler teachers. This shift in perspective and preparation would also benefit teachers working with older children, as the element of care is far too often removed from formal schooling.

IN CONCLUSION

Infant and toddler care and education stands apart from the field of early child care and education at large, which is both a benefit and a disadvantage. The infant and toddler years are unique as the foundational beginning of the life span and critical period for brain development. At the same time, infants and toddlers are taken for granted in education, as the "teaching" of our very youngest children does and must look different than that of their older counterparts. As I illustrated in the stories in this chapter, even where early childhood teaching certifications include teaching children from birth, infant and toddler teaching is seen as inferior to teaching in preschool and the primary grades. Society, in general, views teachers of young children as inconsequential.

In putting forth recommendations to bolster the knowledge base of the field with more classroom-based research and to increase infant/toddler content in teacher preparation programs, my hope is that these inextricably linked pieces will inform policy and raise the visibility and status of infant/toddler teachers. There is much undoing to be done in the ways teachers of very young children have come to be constructed and thus neglected in our society. These on-the-ground changes in research, practice, and teacher education must mirror shifts in policy that support this work.

REFERENCES

Grumet, M. R. (1988). *Bitter milk: Women and teaching.* University of Massachusetts Press.

McLean, C., Austin, L. J. E., Whitebook, M., & Olson, K. L. (2021). *Early childhood workforce index 2020.* Center for the Study of Child Care Employment.

CHAPTER 9

Recognizing the Birth-to-3 Workforce as Educators

Emily Sharrock and Annie Schaeffing

As the other chapters in this section remind us, early childhood educators care for children during a crucial time in their development, when responsive, consistent relationships create a foundation for future success in school, relationships, and life. Our brains grow explosively during the first 3 years of life, developing more than 1 million neural connections a second (Center on the Developing Child, 2022). Despite the mounting evidence of the importance of infancy and early childhood, many consider these educators to be "just babysitters." With this comes a lack of investment in the workforce, resulting in low pay and lack of benefits for a field made up of approximately 40 percent women of color (Austin et al., 2019). We can find the roots of this misperception in persistent racism and the history of enslaved women being forced to care for white babies and toddlers (Lloyd et al., 2021). In order to respect the educators who do this vital work, we must invest in our early childhood system in the same way we do our K–12 system—by treating it as a public good and creating the conditions for well-paid and well-prepared teachers.

INEQUITIES BY THE NUMBERS

The United States falls behind other wealthy nations on spending for early childhood, with less than 20% of total public spending on family benefits and education going toward birth to 5-year-olds. Early childhood educators in the United States are paid so poorly that nearly half of them rely on public assistance. Caitlin McLean and her colleagues (2021) have found that 86% percent earn less than $15 per hour, and only 15% receive employer-sponsored health insurance. Compensation for this workforce has increased by only 1% in the past 25 years (Whitebook et al., 2014).

While K–12 teacher salaries also deserve to be higher, they average $59,420 and include comprehensive benefits packages, and 84% of the K–12 workforce is white (Bureau of Labor Statistics, 2019; National Center for Education Statistics, 2018). Significant wage disparities also exist within the field, which is made up of 40% women of color who are clustered primarily in the lower-wage jobs, such as aides and assistants (Austin et al., 2019). Nationally, on average, Black female educators working full-time in settings that serve children ages birth–5 make 84 cents for every $1 earned by their white counterparts (Ullrich et al., 2016). This 16% gap means that a Black teacher would make $366 less per month and $4,392 less per year, on average, than their white counterparts—despite often having deeper cultural knowledge and better reflecting the children they serve.

If infant/toddler educators earn a bachelor's degree and decide to transition to teaching prekindergarten in a state-funded program, which often requires BA degrees, they can move from poverty wages to making a middle-class salary at parity with elementary school teachers. While providing an important opportunity for proper compensation, this further bifurcates the field between those teaching children from birth to age 3 and those teaching 4- and 5-year-olds.

Investments in professional learning offer another example of these disparities. The United States currently spends about $18 billion annually on professional development for educators in public K–12 schools, which translates to approximately $5,625 per teacher per year (National Center for Education Statistics, 2019). Even if states allocated their entire allowable federal allocation from the Child Care Development Block Grant (CCDBG) quality set-aside pool (child care funding that goes to states and is earmarked for quality improvement efforts), it would only translate to $234 per educator each year for professional learning, 20 times less than is spent on professional learning for educators in the K–12 system (National Academies of Sciences, Engineering, and Medicine, 2018). While the K–12 school system also lacks needed resources required to provide high-quality education to all children, the system is still funded significantly better than the early years system and at a lower percentage of overall education spending when compared to other industrialized countries (Figure 9.1).

INVESTING IN EDUCATORS

To resolve these inequities, society at large must recognize that child care is more than just a safe place for children to go when parents are working. As several chapters in this volume stress, early childhood educators require specific skills and competencies to provide high-quality care. They must have access to professional development that centers on topics such as establishing supportive relationships with children and families, creating learning environments that cultivate exploration and discovery, and facilitating interactions with and among children. Professional learning models

Figure 9.1. Comparative Funding, by Age (United States)/United States and Selected Nations

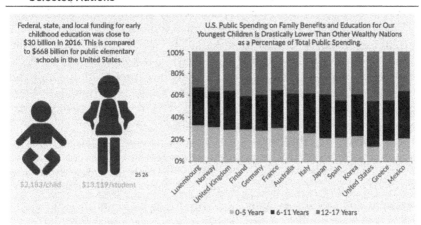

Federal, state, and local funding for early childhood education was close to $30 billion in 2016. This is compared to $668 billion for public elementary schools in the United States.

U.S. Public Spending on Family Benefits and Education for Our Youngest Children is Drastically Lower Than Other Wealthy Nations as a Percentage of Total Public Spending.

■ 0-5 Years ■ 6-11 Years ■ 12-17 Years

(Sharrock & Parkerson, 2020; data sources: National Academies of Sciences, Engineering, and Medicine, 2018; National Center for Education Statistics, 2019; OECD, 2017

can be designed with flexibility for those who are currently working or at a more intensive pace for educators who are preparing to (re)enter the workforce. States can pay a stipend for participation in professional learning and align programs to locally adopted competencies, licensing, and credential requirements.

Partnerships with community colleges can bring professional learning programs to scale and enable the provision of college credits upon completion. A system of tailored professional learning that is anchored in the principles of adult development, including job-embedded learning experiences such as mentoring and coaching, can both improve program quality and support increased teacher retention and job satisfaction, thus further contributing to the stable caregiver relationships on which healthy child development depends. These kinds of investments and strategies are doable and within reach for states and communities now.

To truly transform the system, more systemic investments are needed to make the shift from treating the workforce as "providers" and instead investing in them as "educators," as we do in the K–12 system. Infant/toddler educators need access to, funding for, and eventually requirements to earn associate and bachelor's degrees in programs that specifically focus on the developmental needs of infants and toddlers and provide fieldwork placements in infant/toddler settings. Due to demand for early childhood degrees primarily for prekindergarten roles, there has not been any incentive to focus on infant/toddler development, and thus investment is needed to enhance the curriculum and expertise of faculty in these programs. Unlike many prospective educators in elementary school degree programs, infant/toddler educators are often enrolling in higher education with years of experience in the field. Therefore, to recognize and build from existing skills and competencies, higher education should offer differentiated opportunities for educators so that they can learn in ways that honor their experience. These efforts will not only better support developmentally meaningful experiences and growth for all children, but will also begin to address long-standing inequity in the early care and education system by honoring educators' time, previous experience, and effort.

Participation in these pathways can pave the way for pay parity with similar elementary school teachers. Parity compensation scales should recognize experience as well as degrees and credentials, honoring those who have been underpaid in the field for decades. This will help to retain existing talent and recruit new educators into the field. Compensation parity for the early care and education workforce is also critical for addressing inequities in the field, ensuring that the primarily Black and Latinx women who care for young children are paid similarly to the majority-white K–12 workforce.

Significant public investment is needed to make these shifts. We estimate that at a national scale, the annual cost of comprehensive compensation reform would cost $40.2 billion, and the annual cost of a residency program with job-embedded coaching would be $2.2 billion (Sharrock & Parkerson, 2020). While expensive, the return on investment is clear. A broad range of data show that every dollar invested in quality early childhood programs yields anywhere between $4 and $21 in return in individual and community outcomes—and the earlier these services begin, the higher the return on investment (Heckman, 2008). The pandemic made clear the costs to communities of neglecting these investments. Many more states and localities are finding creative ways to raise revenue, such as DC's tax increase on high earners, which will enable implementation of a parity compensation scale, as well as San Francisco's Commercial Rent Tax, which will provide annual salary increases of $8,000 to $30,000 per educator (San Francisco Office of Early Care & Education, 2022; Sproul & Sklar, 2022).

As these shifts are made, careful attention to devising the right strategies for strong system-building is crucial. For example, more states have been moving toward paying subsidy rates that reflect the cost of quality instead of market rates, which frequently undercuts what is necessary to provide a living wage. Contracted models are another promising approach, especially when used in child care deserts. Contracts pay child care subsidies to providers based on enrollment rather than child attendance and can provide a consistent funding flow to child care providers that enable them to pay their employees a higher wage.

To build a truly equitable, stable early care and education system, we need to create lasting systems and structures that will sustain guaranteed access to developmentally meaningful experiences for all children and families beginning at birth. This begins with recognizing the value of, and investing in, our workforce for the long term.

REFERENCES

Austin, L.J.E., Edwards, B., & Whitebook, M. (2019, December 19). *Racial wage gaps in early education employment*. Center for the Study of Child Care Employment.

Bureau of Labor Statistics. (2019). *Kindergarten and elementary teachers*. https://www.bls.gov/ooh/education-training-and-library/kindergarten-and-.elementary-school-teachers.htm

Center on the Developing Child. (2022). *Brain architecture*. https://developingchild.harvard.edu/science/key-concepts/brain-architecture/

Heckman, J. (2008). Schools, skills, and synapses. *Economic Inquiry, 46*(3), 289–324.

Lloyd, C. M., Carlson, J., Barnett, H., Shaw, S., & Logan, D. (2021). *Mary Pauper: A historical exploration of early care and education compensation, policy, and solutions*. Child Trends.

McLean, C., Austin, L. J. E. Whitebook, M., & Olson, K. L. (2021). *Early childhood workforce index 2020*. Center for the Study of Child Care Employment.

National Academies of Sciences, Engineering, and Medicine. (2018). *Transforming the financing of early care and education*. The National Academies Press.

National Center for Education Statistics. (2018). *Characteristics of public school teachers*. https://nces.ed.gov/programs/coe/indicator/clr/public-school-teachers

National Center for Education Statistics. (2019). *Public school expenditures*. https://nces.ed.gov/programs/coe/indicator_cmb.asp

OECD. (2017). *PF1.6B Public spending by age of children* (2011 data). https://www.oecd.org/els/family/PF1_6_Public_spending_by_age_of_children.pdf

San Francisco Office of Early Care & Education. (2020). *Landmark pay raise initiative for early educators in city-funded programs*. https://sfoece.org/2022/05/04/landmark-pay-raise-initiative-for-early-educators-in-city-funded-programs/

Sharrock, E., & Parkerson, C. (2020). *Investing in the birth-to-three workforce: A new vision to strengthen the foundation for all learning*. Bank Street College of Education.

Sproul, J., & Sklar, C. (2022, February 22). *D.C. leads the way to increased pay for infant and toddler teachers*. https://www.newamerica.org/education-policy/edcentral/dc-leads-the-way-to-increased-pay-for-infant-and-toddler-teachers/#:~:text=In%20early%20February%2C%20based%20on,Childhood%20Educator%20Pay%20Equity%20Fund

Ullrich, R., Hamm, K., & Herzfeldt-Kamprath, R. (2016). *Underpaid and unequal*. Center for American Progress.

Whitebook, M., Howes, C., & Phillips, D. (2014). *Worthy work, still unlivable wages*. Center for the Study of Child Care Employment.

Part IV

DE/PROFESSIONALIZATION

The implications of not having a cohesive workforce due to systemic barriers (such as pay disparities) and inequitable access to teacher education result in competition, individualization, and systems fragmentation. Structures that uphold prevailing ideas on what it means to be a professional are reinforced by whiteness, racism, and patriarchy. As the essays in this section convey, these must be dismantled and dispelled by people's collective efforts toward justice, the power of diversity, and expanding how qualifications for professionals must encompass experience, care, community, and connection.

The contributors to this section underscore the need to involve early childhood community members—notably people working in a range of early care and education settings—in discussions and shared decision-making around credentialing and professionalization, teacher education and professional learning, and quality improvement. Lea Austin outlines the issues that have fueled the de/professionalization movements in recent years. Members of the Brooklyn Coalition of Early Childhood Programs, Juliana Pinto McKeen, Fabiola Santos-Gaerlan, Alice Tse Chiu, and Wendy Jo Cole, reflect on their experiences in early childhood leadership and the issues they have faced with regard to hiring within the parameters of quality improvement initiatives. Betzaida Vera-Heredia concludes this section by offering a series of recommendations for being more expansive in our thinking around professionalization.

CHAPTER 10

Grounding Educators' Experiences, Perspectives, and Intellect in De/Professionalization Debates

Lea J. E. Austin

The longstanding debates about whether and how to professionalize the early care and education workforce were not brewed up in a 21st-century framework, but have been simmering—and sometimes boiling over—for more than a century. Is it more care or education? Just how much training or education is enough to do this work? To degree or not to degree? Will changes to workforce requirements change the face of the workforce? How will any of these decisions professionalize the workforce?

Deeply rooted values about who performs care and early education work and what the work involves frame these debates on the pages of academic papers, at policy tables, and in the halls of government. Having closely watched, and sometimes participated myself, I've observed that more often than not, the debaters are themselves well educated, decently (if not well) paid, and for the most part white. The early childhood workers in question are rarely sought out as experts or welcomed into these debates, and the long tradition of Black women leading in this space has been obscured (Williams, 2022).

(DE)VALUING THE WORKFORCE

Care and early education—work performed almost exclusively by women—have long been devalued in our country. For proof, we need only look at recent history. At the onset of the COVID-19 pandemic, public schools and entire communities closed, yet most child care remained open. State and local governments expected and even encouraged this response, yet with the exception of a handful of states, there was no hazard or "shero" pay, and few distributions of personal protective equipment in the first uncertain and frightening months. One state even noted in their health guidance that if child care workers could not access protective equipment like gowns, they should wear garbage bags (State of Illinois, Governor's Office of Early Childhood Development, 2020, pg. 8). Garbage bags! A more humane response would have been to provide the financial resources that would allow child care programs to temporarily close until it was safe to resume work.

With little to no help in sight, it took only months for child care and its workforce to be on the brink of collapse. By July 2020, one in five child care providers in California, for example, had already fallen behind on the mortgage or rent for their businesses, and in the fall of 2020, one-third were food-insecure (Powell et al., 2022). All the while, in a bid to recruit and retain workers, corporations like Walmart, Target, and Starbucks raised entry-level wages to at least double the median wage of child care workers, and public schools offered degreed teachers signing bonuses and pay bumps. It's no wonder that by Year 2 of the pandemic, even after financial relief finally came, America's early care and education system had lost 131,000 workers (Center for the Study of Child Care Employment [CSCCE], 2022).

Considering these conditions, the question of what or whether certain qualifications or standards (de)professionalize this workforce is far removed from the modern context of what it means to be an early educator. How can a single degree or set of qualifications or standards for workers change how this workforce is treated?

Across the country, policies are laden with values about who is capable of teaching young children and the measure of their worth. Those who teach preschool children are paid more than infant and toddler teachers, and preschool teachers who work in public school settings are paid more than other preschool teachers. A closer look at data and policy reveals that simply setting up pathways to those best-paying jobs or mirroring standards across the sector is not the singular solution. Black preschool teachers, for example, are systematically paid less than their peers, to the tune of $3,600 a year, even when they have the same level of education (Austin et al., 2019).

The devaluation of early educators' experiences and education is built into policy. In California, for example, when the state established universal, school-based preschool for 4-year-olds, there was no way to become a teacher in the program without a credential that has very little, if any, early-childhood-related content or pedagogy. Early educators with bachelor's and even master's degrees in early childhood education and 10 years of experience teaching young children were deemed less qualified in the eyes of the state than someone with a bachelor's degree in a completely unrelated topic (anthropology, for example) and no experience teaching preschool age children or younger, but who had completed a traditional credential program. Early educators would have to leave

their jobs to fulfill the student teaching requirement to become creden-
tialed, yet alternative pathways exist for those preparing to become K–12
teachers. Strikingly, more than two-thirds of California's early education
workforce are people of color, while nearly two-thirds of its K–12 teachers are white.

Rather than continue to host debates *about* the workforce from privi-
leged positions, a more productive question would be, What do early educators *themselves* identify as needs in order to thrive in their work?

GROUNDED POLICY

In research, constructivist grounded theory is an approach by which theories are filtered through experiences and interactions with people and perspectives. This approach requires the researcher to acknowledge they hold
biases and to check and confront those biases in the process of the research. Constructivist grounded theory rejects the presupposition that the
researcher is the authority who develops their own theory and then seeks
to prove or disprove it through research. What if policy took a similar
approach and we sought to construct grounded policies? How would the
debate questions be posed differently if educators asked them?

Since its founding in 1999, the Center for the Study of Child Care
Employment (CSCCE), where I now work, has been learning from and with
early educators about their experiences, practices, needs, and desires. It is
no coincidence that CSCCE was founded by a former infant and toddler
teacher and worthy wage activist Marcy Whitebook. A series of salary surveys conducted by educators themselves across the country led to the first
National Child Care Staffing study, a series of teacher-helmed advocacy
organizations, and eventually the creation of CSCCE, a home for research
focused solely on this workforce.

Decades of research and engagement with educators reveal findings that
are seemingly straightforward, yet continue to be neglected in policy.

Preparation

Educators want and need the appropriate conditions to access and engage in good preparation and ongoing learning. They require conditions
that support their success and remove barriers that have historically undermined college attainment for people of color, immigrants, and working women. Scholarships are a critical resource, but interviews and surveys
with educators reveal that additional resources like cohorts, academic supports, community-located and hybrid–virtual coursework, and systems innovations like apprenticeship models also support education attainment
(Copeman Petig et al., 2019; Whitebook et al., 2011). Notably, degree

completion rates in programs for early educators that offer these supports are higher than for the general student population.

Educators need to be recognized as capable of and interested in building their knowledge and skills. Taking only one or two classes at a time or skipping terms is not about motivation or commitment. When educators are asked, we learn that these patterns are often linked to scarce resources, work and family responsibilities, and barriers in systems designed to exclude them. Critically, when making policy decisions about qualifications, systems and policy leaders should check their own biases and assumptions about the capacity of early educators to succeed. While I routinely hear concerns that setting education requirements or raising qualifications will whiten the workforce, this is rarely followed by strategizing on how to translate existing experience and training into qualifications and provide the resources and conditions for the diversity of our current and future workforce to be successful.

How would education and qualification policy shift if educators were actively involved in decision making?

Working Conditions

Educators need safe, supportive working environments, including paid time to do all the things they need to do besides teach (i.e., plan curriculum, complete assessment, meet with teaching teams, communicate with parents). Children's learning environments are their teachers' working environments. Yet the conditions and practices in the workplace that support educators to effectively facilitate children's learning and development receive little attention. While quality rating and improvement systems (QRIS) have become the dominant strategy for addressing program improvement, most are silent on indicators of quality work environments for the adults (McLean et al., 2021). Instead, the emphasis is on observing and measuring their practices and counting levels of education. This approach fails to recognize the role that working conditions play in quality. No matter how good their education and training, quality is undermined if working conditions sabotage educators' ability to apply their knowledge.

In 2014, the International Labour Organization (ILO) published the *ILO Policy Guidelines on the Promotion of Decent Work for Early Childhood Education Personnel* to articulate standards for the work environments of early educators. The ILO standards include staffing levels, paid professional time, leadership and mentoring, and compensation (ILO, 2014). As of 2022, no federal or state agency regulating early care and education in the United States had taken up the ILO standards. But there is no need to even look abroad for guidance. Even before the QRIS movement, early educators themselves engaged in an extensive process to articulate Model

Work Standards for center- and home-based programs and published them in a manner that would easily translate into quality indicators and quality improvement plans (CSCCE, 2019). Yet the Model Work Standards were mostly ignored as systems administrators and policy leaders developed QRIS. What would quality improvement systems look like if educators were actively shaping standards and quality indicators?

Compensation

Educators need appropriate compensation so that they can support themselves and their own families without worrying about how to pay bills or put food on the table. Three decades ago, the first National Child Care Staffing Study linked poor wages and turnover to poor quality (Whitebook et al., 1989). Today, early educators continue to experience poverty at double the rate of other workers and are among the lowest-paid workers in every state (McLean et al., 2021).

Such economic hardship not only undermines educators' ability to deliver on the promise of high-quality early care and education, it also harms those performing this work and their own families. Furthermore, such low pay is at odds with the complex skills and knowledge required to effectively foster the learning and development of young children. In several studies, my research team and I have asked educators a simple question: "What do you want people to know about being an early educator?" Their thousands of responses demonstrate the human toll these conditions have had. No one working to care for and educate children should be worried about how to feed their own families. They should be able to perform this essential service without trading off their own well-being.

How would compensation policies be developed and prioritized among broader early care and education policies if educators were actively constructing policy?

CONCLUSION

There is a pressing need to center the workforce—their singular (narrative) and collective (quantitative) data and their ideas for change—in policy across all levels of government. There is no question that we need policy change. Will policies be a response to debates posed by elites? Or will policies be grounded in educators' experiences, perspectives, intellect, and expertise?

I assume good intent among the great debaters, but ultimately, it's the outcomes that matter. Good intent is not a salve for outcomes that are harmful, demoralizing, and oppressive. When our early care and education workforce policies come *from* educators, they will be *for* educators and reflect the preparation, conditions, and compensation aligned with their profession of teaching and caring for our youngest children.

REFERENCES

Austin, L. J. E., Edwards, B., Chávez, R., & Whitebook, M. (2019). *Racial wage gaps in early education employment*. Center for the Study of Child Care Employment.

Center for the Study of Child Care Employment (CSCCE). (2022). *Child care sector jobs BLS analysis*. https://cscce.berkeley.edu/child-care-sector-jobs-bls-analysis/

Copeman Petig, A., Chávez, R., & Austin, L. J. E. (2019). *Strengthening the knowledge, skills, and professional identity of early educators*. Center for the Study of Child Care Employment.

CSCCE. (2019). *Model work standards*. https://cscce.berkeley.edu/publications/report/creating-better-child-care-jobs-model-work-standards/

International Labour Office (ILO), Sectoral Activities Department. (2014). *ILO policy guidelines on the promotion of decent work for early childhood education personnel*. International Labour Office.

McLean, C., Austin, L. J. E., Whitebook, M., & Olson, K. L. (2021). *Early childhood workforce index 2020*. Center for the Study of Child Care Employment.

Powell, A., Chávez, R., Austin, L. J. E., Montoya, E., Kim, Y., & Copeman Petig, A. (2022). *"The forgotten ones."* Center for the Study of Child Care Employment.

State of Illinois, Governor's Office of Early Childhood Development. (2020, May 11). *Emergency child care FAQs*. https://www2.illinois.gov/sites/OECD/Documents/Emergency%20Child%20Care%20FAQs%20200511_final.pdf

Whitebook, M., Howes, C., & Phillips, D. (1989). *Who cares? Child care teachers and quality of care in America*. Child Care Employee Project.

Whitebook, M., Kipnis, F., Sakai, L., & Almaraz, M. (2011). *Learning together*. Center for the Study of Child Care Employment.

Williams, R. E. (2022). Josephine Silone Yates: Pedagogical giant and organizational leader in early education and beyond (Profiles in Early Education Leadership, No. 3). Center for the Study of Child Care Employment.

CHAPTER 11

Toward Equity in Professionalization Through Community- and Coalition-Building

Juliana Pinto McKeen, Fabiola Santos-Gaerlan, Alice Tse Chiu, and Wendy Jo Cole

We are writing as child care directors, owners, workers, and advocates. We came together in March 2020 to form the Brooklyn Coalition of Early Childhood Programs (BCECP), when the COVID-19 pandemic began, in an effort to survive and support our diverse programs and one another. As we worked together, we began to imagine and practice what a society would be like that supports child care and the underpaid, undervalued workers whom we know are essential. Who are these workers, including us? And how does our field, through professionalization or deprofessionalization, support children, families, and those who give decades of their lives to nurturing, educating, and raising other people's children? We found a tension here, often seen in the "we are not just babysitters" language. We are caregivers, we are educators, we value the both/and.

We want to begin by sharing insights into who we are and what we need from a broad anti-racist, decolonized, inclusive perspective. This means reflecting deeply on these tensions in relation to both professionalization and deprofessionalization, including:

- wisdom/experience versus education;
- access, specifically access to education for Black and Brown teachers; and
- policies surrounding professionalization/deprofessionalization such as access to funding, support, and growth.

Our hope in this praxis is to further our field in valuing and supporting every single member of the early childhood community and working toward a vision of integrity and a true support of an anti-racist, decolonized, inclusive early childhood.

WISDOM VERSUS EDUCATION IN HIRING

I (Alice) remember dropping my son off on his very first day of preschool. He was terrified, as was I. The teachers seemed very eager to introduce him to the classroom and get him acclimated to the environment. This didn't stop him from continuing to cry for 8 months, every time I brought him to school.

I forgot his lunch box one day and returned with it about an hour later. I peeked through the window and observed my son sitting on a chair, crying in a corner. A teacher was sitting beside him with her arm around his shoulders but not actually touching his body. Only her fingers were gently tapping his shoulder. I was horrified and disappointed. Did she not understand that holding him and giving him deep hugs to console him would help ease his nervousness? Did she not understand that speaking to him, talking to him about his feelings, validating them, and reassuring him everything would be okay would be comforting? The teacher simply sat there and allowed him to continue to cry.

Years later, after transitioning out of a successful career as a pediatric therapist, remembering my son's experience, I opened an intimate neighborhood preschool. I wanted to hire teachers who would genuinely love to hold and hug and who had a true desire to be with children. Teachers who would giggle with delight at all the children's achievements. Educators who had an innate sense and actually spoke the same "language" as the children.

Sadly, I found the city regulations were extremely restrictive about whom I may hire. In our city, approved teachers must have a degree in education specifically; no other education background is acceptable. This meant that my 20+ years working with special children in early childhood education did not allow me to teach the children in my school. It is important to note that all children are special, but these children are special in their own way, not "typical." They are "able," just not able in the way one would typically define it.

There are many challenges to hiring teachers who have certification *and* an intrinsic sense in caring for children. Many certified teachers I've met may have somehow completed the educational requirements, but don't seem to have the patience, the care, the experience, the genuine love to be with children. Teaching is the act of encouraging learning through activities and discovery. Who better to do this than a person who has acquired wisdom through years of being present with children, and/or simply is intuitive, and has the natural ability to truly understand and respect the child? Why must the teacher, especially for such a young age, be a certified educator, with no thought with regard to their life experience or instinctive beliefs and behaviors?

In a survey presented to over 50 BCECP early childhood directors in the winter of 2021, all who responded agreed that having teachers who are wise is more important and more valuable than someone with a formal education. More value must be placed on an individual's experience and wisdom with regard to working with children. Anything can be taught, but wisdom is often an inborn trait or gained through many years of experience.

"PROFESSIONAL" LEARNING AND PATHWAYS TO LEADERSHIP

I (Fabiola) was a television producer for 15 years before I opened my home day care in Brooklyn. I grew up in the Philippines, where I dreamed of being a poet and a filmmaker, and came to New York at 18 years old. Producing and directing was an abridged, evolved version of that dream, and I obtained my master's of fine arts in Television Production through a sponsored program.

Truthfully, I didn't want children in my 20s. I myself didn't have the most fulfilling childhood, as my mother left me in the care of my grandmother when she moved to America, as many Filipino parents did. When I had two children in my 30s, I had learned enough about myself by then to know I wanted to be a mindful, attentive, and supportive parent. Raising my children, I was intentional about our communication and the things they were learning from me. Now I know that was the kindling to my passion for early childhood education. I raised my children the way I would have wanted to be raised.

I never did finish my early childhood education degree. Between tending my family and operating my business, I couldn't afford the cost and the time of school. To supplement, I attended education professional conferences by every organization from Bank Street to NAEYC, but of course, I still had to hire an education director with a degree. I couldn't direct my own business.

Now, 22 years later, as I hire staff for my three child care centers, I very intentionally balance the variety of experience in my teachers between the Education Director, the nurturing teacher, and the energetic and fun teacher. For my infant/toddler programs, I have mothers who will rock and hug teary toddlers until they're settled. They are good at that because they have had the best training: the commitment of caring for their own children.

Being Brown and female was not easy in the TV industry. I wrestled my way up to being a producer and director, often working with people less educated than I was. Growing my own child care business was just as difficult, even though it was mine. I felt isolated from the business community, and information and guidance weren't accessible. The agencies I had to collaborate with—like the Department of Buildings, the Fire Department, and the Department of Health—were often punitive. I felt denied before I made a request, unwanted, unsupported, and conspired against by indecipherable rules, impossible requirements, and deficient resources. Everything was harder than it should have been.

The contrast between the ease of corporate life producing TV fluff and the hardships of operating a service that helps families and children survive in a chaotic, unaccommodating world is so stark. Our industry's desperation during the COVID-19 pandemic really accentuated how priorities are misaligned. One of the most essential services to a functional society is undervalued and neglected.

Adding the context of being a Brown woman in the child care industry, and America, and 2022, every day feels like a battle for respect and consideration. It's won every time a parent comes to pick up a healthy and happy child.

POLICIES OF PROFESSIONALIZATION

I (Juliana) believe that caregiving is a human trait. Some of us may be more inclined to do it, but at some point in all our lives, we have needed and will need care. Changes in the field of early childhood care and education over the past few decades have tended to favor higher education for caregivers, thus professionalizing caregiving. Policies mandating higher levels of education to secure employment in early learning programs may have come from a place of goodwill. However, the impact of these policies is different from the supposed intention. The impact includes whitewashing of the profession; decreasing access to the field for lower-income, Black, and Brown caregivers; and an increase of bureaucracy for both individuals and programs. As a BCECP member responded in the Winter 2021 BCECP survey, "Professionalization can come with a varnish of respect." This is not to say that respect for higher education is not merited, but it simultaneously creates a dichotomy between the haves and the have-nots. Those who do not have a certificate or diploma certifying their knowledge may still be excellent caregivers and educators. However, they are often excluded from jobs or higher wages and considered less valuable than folks who do have that diploma.

Programs whose educators have more education are eligible for more public funding, thus increasing the gaps between those who have access to this education and those who do not. Like many other aspects of our society, those who have access tend to succeed and earn more exponentially, while those who do not have access tend to earn less and are pushed out of the space over time. Policies that require higher education for early education have a hand in policing the profession, edging out Black, Brown, low-income, and disabled caregivers.

Perhaps policymakers believed that higher levels of education in the field would make programs better. However, respondents to our survey seemed to believe that higher education does not make a better educator. We can teach adults how to plan lessons and make materials for an early childhood classroom, but we cannot make them have a passion for it. We cannot substitute theory for practice and the innate wisdom some caregivers have. Respondents of our survey have to grapple with hiring someone who has wisdom and ideally also the higher education to meet employment requirements tied to licensure and funding.

The question remains: Do these policies make the field of early childhood education better? We posit that as they are written and enforced now, they do not. They increase red tape for programs and educators, make hiring more difficult, and deny access to passionate and wise educators who cannot afford the time or tuition money to enroll in higher education so they can be hired at an early education program.

CHAPTER 12

Toward Professionalization *By* the People

Betzaida Vera-Heredia

My journey in the early childhood care and education field began over 20 years ago. My first professional experience was as an outreach specialist providing services and resources to Spanish-speaking "child care providers" and supporting them in navigating the regulatory system in the state of Wisconsin. The cohorts consisted of Spanish-speaking participants with quite diverse backgrounds and experiences.

Few had previously completed child development education and training in their home countries. For many others, the early childhood field was one they never thought they would work in, but it was considered an easy entry-level job. Some participants had strong literacy skills in Spanish but not so in English. Many others had limited literacy in Spanish and none in English. Regardless of their literacy skills and reasons for working in the field, almost all found the rules, regulations, and requirements confusing or difficult to attain. This confusion was particularly true when the educational requirements slowly changed from professional development hours to college-level credit requirements.

I witnessed how new regulations impacted the life of Spanish-speaking practitioners. As the cohorts moved on and forward and gained experiences and acquired skills, I accepted other positions that allowed me to continue supporting them in their journeys. One of these positions was as a part-time faculty instructor for a technical college. The courses that I initially taught were in the continuing education program, explicitly intended for students interested in obtaining credentials and moving up in the career lattice.

When I facilitated these courses, I intentionally did so to prepare students for the new educational changes and requirements coming down the nationwide pipeline. Only a handful could cope with the level of rigor without assistance. The majority needed significant educational support. The overarching educational goal was to successfully prepare students to complete advanced courses, including college-level courses. Twenty years ago, students and faculty colleagues did not understand or welcome this visionary goal. The main argument against it was that supporting students to develop critical thinking skills or preparing students for advanced courses was not what they needed.

Regardless of the opposition, I was particularly excited about the changes and how these could professionalize the field and elevate the status from "child care providers" to "early childhood educators." I was excited, but my excitement was not necessarily shared or experienced the same way by the students. As time passed, the Spanish-speaking early childhood educators whom I met and who decided to stay working in the field became more versed, better understood the system, and learned how to *survive* in it. I would ask them if they understood the current educational and training requirements. The majority shared that they understood the requirements and the "good intentions" behind them; however, they did not know how they would meet them.

STAYING THE COURSE DESPITE ISSUES THAT PERSIST OVER TIME

More than 20 years later, after meeting with the first cohort of Spanish-speaking early childhood educators, many still share a concern about not having the academic English comprehension and literacy skills to understand the content of advanced and college-level courses. These educators have stayed in the field for more than 2 decades. The educators have taken additional steps to position themselves better and continue in business. Some have completed continuing education courses to improve their literacy skills in Spanish with parents or courses to learn basic English to better communicate with licensors when they visit their programs.

Completing continuing education courses requires a different effort than completing courses for college credit. The levels of rigor are different, with college courses requiring more time studying and completing assignments. It is assumed that students in higher education programs have acquired the level of literacy skills needed to satisfactorily complete college-level courses prior to enrollment. As mentioned earlier, not all educators would have the literacy skills needed to satisfactorily complete college-level courses.

Educators are aware that the investment of their time and effort is significantly higher for completing college-level courses. So the questions many of them have are: who will support them, and how will the support be delivered? Is the expectation that educators will spend their evenings and weekends attending classes? If the expectation is that educators will attend sessions during the day, who would care for the children in their programs?

Perhaps an even greater reason for not meeting the educational requirement is not having the financial resources to cover related costs. Educators have provided the best care and education they could throughout the years. The love for and commitment to young children and their families are undeniable. However, this has not translated into higher wages or access to financial resources that would fully cover all expenses directly or indirectly related to completing higher education programs. Educators have endured complicated and challenging situations such as the national financial crisis, changes in child care subsidies, and a global pandemic. Even though educators are still struggling to make ends meet, they continue in the field.

MOVING FROM POLICIES *DONE TO* PEOPLE
TO POLICIES *MADE WITH* PEOPLE

Early childhood educators continue providing care and education to our youngest citizens while facing changes in policies and regulations without a clear understanding of the policymaking process. Almost all the students and colleagues that I have met have answered "no" when asked if they know or understand the policy changes or development that have resulted in the current educational requirements. Frequently, educators do not even know who in their cities, districts, counties, and states is responsible for representing them when developing policies that directly impact their well-being. This situation is not unique to the early childhood care and education field, but is one more example of policies *done to people, not with people.* It is another example of top-down decisions that impact the lives of people whose voices were not heard or acknowledged during the policymaking process. It is an example of policies that do not acknowledge educators' funds of knowledge, passion, and commitment to the early childhood field, whose values and beliefs are not consistently recognized in college-level curricula.

The newly imposed policies are often well intended. It is understood—or assumed—that highly educated early childhood educators will provide the utmost-quality care and education to young children. Learning about child development theory and promising practices would expand the educators' understanding of how to best meet the needs of young children and their families and how to best support their development holistically.

It is also assumed that the higher the level of educational achievements the workforce achieves, the more the level of professionalism of the early childhood educators will also increase. In turn, a higher level of professionalism will support efforts toward professionalizing the field. Nonetheless, the issue of fulfillment remains. The current policies are significantly challenging to comply with, not because of a lack of interest or willingness, but because the system does not provide the support and resources needed to achieve the requirements and expectations embedded in the policies. However, there are opportunities to remedy the issues with existing policies. The following are recommendations to address the issues related to compliance:

- Investing in educators by offering continuing ed programs and high-quality professional development opportunities to prepare educators to complete college degrees is imperative. Educators should have access to a comprehensive support system that includes tutors, mentors, and coaches and access to libraries, educational resources, and technology. Educators need a robust support system that will ensure an adequate understanding of the content and how to effectively and intentionally transfer the knowledge acquired into their daily practice.
- Removing barriers for all educators to access higher education without impacting their finances. If providing scholarships to *all* early childhood educators is not possible, then financial assistance programs should be created to aid *all* educators. Financial assistance programs must offer reasonable and compassionate options for repayment, forbearance, and debt forgiveness. Institutions providing loans must acknowledge the specific characteristics of the early childhood workforce and must consider them when establishing repayment options.
- Rethinking hiring processes by easing requirements and establishing professional development programs to support educators in completing educational requirements. It is known that early childhood programs face financial hardships when their budget depends solely or mainly on tuition. Therefore, it is imperative to find external funds to cover costs related to professional development plans and staff retention. Professional development plans should be individualized and congruent with on-hand teacher development and the programs where educators work.
- Decentralizing policymaking processes. Effective and well-coordinated efforts should be implemented to ensure that educators at all levels have access to participate or contribute to policymaking processes. This should not be done behind closed doors. Educators must be aware and informed about new policies or changes to existing policies before they impact their livelihoods.

The field needs a competent and well-educated workforce. However, such a workforce will not be achieved if policies are not crafted and implemented in ways that best address the needs and reality of early childhood educators. Therefore, policies should focus on supporting the workforce in professionalizing the early childhood education field instead of policing and penalizing it.

Part V

SUPPORTING THRIVING TEACHERS

The preceding essays have explicitly and implicitly discussed the marginal status of "care teachers" within early child care and education systems that are pervaded by intersecting racism, sexism, and classism. This section builds on those that came before by providing illustrations of creating humanizing spaces for teachers so that they can thrive. In the first chapter, Vanessa Rodriguez reflects on her journey to professional selfhood and the implications of what she has learned about transforming the profession. Abbi Kruse follows by sharing her philosophy for creating a nurturing early years program and how she used social media to create Essential, Not Expendable, an 8,000-strong group of educators who organized, like the Brooklyn Coalition of Early Childhood Programs (Part IV), to weather the COVID-19 pandemic but has become an ongoing space of support and shared wisdom. Lori Falchi and Cristina Medellin-Paz end this section by sharing their work helping teachers to navigate sometimes dehumanizing professionalization systems and how their shared journeys help teachers find their professional voices.

CHAPTER 13

Don't Train Me to Serve!
Supporting Thriving Teachers Through Identity Development

Vanessa Rodriguez

I often wonder how I wound up here. How did I become a researcher? My passion and deep love have always been for teaching children, so why did I leave the classroom? For me the buildup was slow and quite painful. Like many teachers of color, I began teaching so that other students would never have to experience the trauma I had as a student. But I found myself unable to shield them from it. My career started just a couple of years before the testing craze of the millennium took hold, which gave me a couple of years to experience democratic schooling and deep project-based teaching.

Then Mayor Michael Bloomberg and Chancellor Joel Klein took over the NYC public schools, making high-stakes testing, private interests, and standardized teaching the new normal. I remember feeling like my creativity was being crushed and my relationships with children devalued. I saw the anxiety grow in them as city and state assessments drew close. I challenged the unethical demands that principals made on staff to meet the department's mandates. Because of this, I hopped around a lot within the NYC Department of Education (DOE), trying to find a school that I could call home, one that would *allow* me to thrive.

I recall a day when I was (yet again) called into my principal's office. She was angry that I had created another project to engage in with my students. As I entered her office filled with beautiful children's books, colorful throw pillows, and blankets strewn across comfy chairs, I remember feeling the discordance between these decorations and the reprimand I knew I was about to receive. Her forehead crinkled and her eyes were noticeably alert as she demanded that I explain why I had chosen to have students design a small business to teach the 13 colonies, American Revolution, and slavery.

Unmoved by my explanation, she said, "At the end of the day, Vanessa, you of all people should understand that we are here to serve children."

That statement pierced me. I had heard it so many times and bristled at the phrase "serve children," but in this instance I just couldn't bear to submit. I took a deep breath, slowly looked down at my forearm, and noticeably rubbed my browned Latina skin. "My ancestors made the decision long ago to stop serving people," I said, "I teach children, I learn with them, but I do not serve them." This response made her visibly angry, and she yelled, "Why must you always insist on creating new projects for students . . . why can't you just follow the scripted DOE curriculum!? You know really smart people create this and you should just follow them!"

It was then that I realized that the system had not been built to support a teacher like me. I wanted to thrive, personally thrive. I knew intuitively that this would benefit my students, but I had no proof, and no support. I then stood up and said, "I'm so sorry. This is all my fault. I realize now that this has been a great misunderstanding. This whole time I thought that *I* was one of those really smart people, so I've been designing projects." I then began to walk out of her office, but before leaving I looked down at the curriculum guide she shook at me. I shared that I was the one hired to write that guide for the DOE. Teachers are often thanked but are rarely named as authors in such publications.

It was continued interactions like these that drove me from the classroom and away from teaching my beloved students. I searched for the school that would *allow* me to thrive, when in reality looking for permission highlights a deeper problem with how I defined teaching and therefore what I was searching for. The dominant narrative is that teachers are *trained* to *serve* children. This behaviorist definition has had far-reaching policy and practice implications for teachers. Notably, its deep historical roots make it especially damaging for women teachers of color.

SELFHOOD ISN'T SELFISH

Teaching isn't a selfless act, as we so often like to proclaim. Rather, it's quite selfish, but in a necessary way. It's a recognition that sharing what we know enables us to coexist with students in ways that support all of our development. Another way to think about this is that individually, humans are not faster, stronger, or smarter than the rest of the animal kingdom, but when we teach one another what we know, we can become stronger, faster, and smarter as a collective mind. Teaching is a survival mechanism.

We need to reimagine how we define teaching if we are to effectively support teachers to thrive. The *simple* act of teaching is not uniquely human, but we are extraordinarily unique in *how* we teach. The how is complex, and what makes us unlike any other animal. As we age and our brains become more sophisticated, we begin to shift our teaching to adjust to our learners' development in relation to our own. The relational development is inextricably linked. However, this is not the definition of teaching used by many teacher education programs or that we hear espoused by policymakers.

Currently, most education efforts center on understanding how *students* learn. Teachers are then told, "Teach this way because that's how *students* learn best." This *student-centered model* focuses on content and behavioral practices, and even in programs that incorporate reflective practice, this is often more about teachers' classroom practice (e.g., lesson plans, student work, content delivery) than on their personal identity development. The problem with this model is that it doesn't take into account how *teachers* learn best, or even that *teachers* are human and not learning tools to be wielded. It doesn't recognize that teaching is developmental for the *teachers* as well.

Teachers develop their ability to teach much like they develop their ability to learn. The most important distinction is that while learning can be an individual act, teaching cannot be done in the absence of at least one student. My students fueled my passion for learning, not just teaching. As a teacher, I was in constant interaction with them—we were developing together.

This relationship requires that teachers be aware of themselves and students at all times. Expecting teachers to be merely learning tools that serve children is requiring that they do not engage in their own learning development. The most significant problem with a service model of teaching is that it is impossible to achieve. It is not possible for teachers to merely enact a scripted curriculum where we serve content to our students like waitresses in a diner. Why, then, have we all been convinced that teaching is unidirectional and subservient?

EARLY YEARS TEACHERS AS WOMEN

It's preferable to envision teachers as serving children because it's a profession dominated by women. Part of the struggle in understanding how to support teachers to thrive in the early years profession is the field's reluctance to acknowledge education's misogynist and racist underpinnings. In the early years, nearly all teachers are women, with urban environments having a prevalence of women of color (Austin et al., 2019). Due to women's dominance in the early years field, it is critical to explore teachers' development through the lens of women as teachers. Self-in-Relation theory (SiR; Miller, 1991), which evolved from feminist research on women's psychological development, emphasizes relationships as the foundation for women's self-identity development. As such, we must consider the unique roles that gender *and* context play in developing teachers' identities. For women teachers, their identities have been formed, in part, by silent, gendered expectations—unspoken agreements that uphold gender hierarchies (Rodriguez et al., 2022).

These expectations regarding how women teachers should care for and interact with students inform how they view themselves and enact their teaching role. Current early years policies have women envisioning themselves as serving rather than learning and developing powerful identities as professionals. SiR theory challenges male-dominant views of development that favor autonomy and separation from caregivers (Surrey, 1985). Instead, women advance their development through a process of growth and relationship-building (Miller, 1991). For example, women develop their teaching skills through understanding their relationships with students—and potentially with one another. *Therefore, teacher development, especially for women, is identity development.* This requires that teachers continually practice self-awareness to be responsive to their students and families.

FIVE AWARENESSES OF TEACHING

Teachers' awareness enables their ability to intentionally and successfully cultivate and practice their identity development. In my work I've developed the Five Awarenesses of Teaching, a comprehensive framework that helps to organize the development of teachers as learners (Rodriguez & Mascio, 2018). The awarenesses include five capacities:

1. Awareness of Self as a Teacher
2. Awareness of Teaching Process
3. Awareness of Learner
4. Awareness of Interaction
5. Awareness of Context

The framework puts forth the understanding that teachers, like their students, are active participants in their own learning and develop skills over time. This is in contrast to a traditional banking model where learners are seen as empty vessels to be filled with knowledge (e.g., scripted teacher training programs). Put simply, a teacher's awarenesses are forever changing, just as humans are forever learning. When we are aware, we can then act with intent.

This is most important to consider if we recognize that we are never teaching the students sitting in our classrooms. Rather, we are teaching who we believe those students to be and who we hope they become. As a teacher, I form hypotheses about my students. I do my best to learn about my students from interactions and observations, but many of my beliefs about students will come from who I am: my values, experiences, and beliefs. Without having an awareness of my "self," I will be misguided in my efforts to teach my students. Teachers who are taught to practice a student-centered model of service, with the belief that they should "check themselves at the door," are at risk of doing harm, to students and themselves, by being unaware of how their personal identities are the most significant factor impacting how they see and, therefore, teach their students. The disconnect often leads to failed interactions between frustrated teachers and students. This kind of self-sacrifice, so commonly expected of women, also denies educators their humanity and right to well-being.

CALL TO ACTION

Historically, our early years policies have required teachers to adhere to male-dominant values of separation and individuality. Our education system lacks a comprehensive understanding of women teachers, how gender and racial identities intersect, and, importantly, their relational development. Consequently, teacher preparation programs, professional development (PD), and teacher evaluations are not grounded in feminist models of teachers' identity development.

We need to invest in novel approaches to professionalization that transcend traditional efforts to modify teacher practice through behavior change. Currently popular strategies serve a patriarchal status quo by promoting that teachers should support themselves, including calls for practicing "self-care" via reflective practices (e.g., meditation) or physical activities (e.g., exercise). Rather than placing the onus on women teachers to take care of themselves, education systems need to accept responsibility for the history of teacher exploitation. Education policies should call for developmentally appropriate supports for teacher learning because it bears repeating that we are human rather than learning tools in service to children.

One way to ensure that we support teachers as human is to implement programming for identity development in parallel to practice-based, student-centered models. For women early years teachers, especially women of color, this can provide a clear pathway toward deconstructing the white male-dominant systems of education. Utilizing tools that are inclusive of feminist theory and that engage trauma-informed processes is critical. The Five Awarenesses of Teaching framework is one place to start (Rodriguez et al., 2020). Others include education journey mapping (Annamma, 2017), whereby teachers create identity maps to explore the cartographies of inequities they've experienced in education and how they have managed to thrive. Affinity healing circles also provide a collective environment for teachers to process trauma while learning from and supporting one another.

Ultimately, tools that directly attend to the teacher as human and support identity development will better position women early years teachers to thrive, not just survive. In turn, they will better support students and families coping with trauma (e.g., racialized). This type of teacher programming and professionalization would be markedly different from practice-based trainings and tools focused on behaviors in service to students. As you read Cristina, Lori, and Abbi's essays in this section, you will see hopeful examples of how supporting thriving teachers can look in action.

REFERENCES

Annamma, S. A. (2017). Cartographies of inequity. In D. Morrison, S. A. Annamma, & D. D. Jackson (Eds.), *Critical race spatial analysis* (pp. 32–50). Stylus.

Austin, L. J. E., Edwards, B., Chávez, R., & Whitebook, M. (2019). *Racial wage gaps in early education employment*. Center for the Study of Child Care Employment.

Miller, J. B. (1991). The development of women's sense of self. In J. V. Jordan, A. G. Kaplan, J. B. Miller, I. P. Stiver, & J. L. Surrey (Eds.), *Women's growth in connection* (pp. 11–26). Guilford Press.

Rodriguez, V., & Mascio, B. (2018). What is the skill of teaching? In A. E. Lopez & E. L. Olan (Eds.), *Transformative pedagogies for teacher education* (pp. 103–122). Information Age Publishing.

Rodriguez, V., Rojas, N. M., Rabadi-Raol, A., Souto-Manning, M. V., & Brotman, L. M. (2022). Silent expectations: An exploration of women pre-kindergarten teachers' mental health and wellness during Covid-19 and beyond. *Early Childhood Research Quarterly, 60*, 80–95.

Rodriguez, V., Solis, S. L., Mascio, B., Kiely Gouley, K., Jennings, P. A., & Brotman, L. M. (2020). With awareness comes competency. *Early Education & Development, 31*(7), 940–972.

Surrey, J. L. (1985). *The self-in-relation*. Stone Center for Developmental Services and Studies.

CHAPTER 14

"I Want to Be Treated Like I'm Valuable"

Advocating for Teachers' Humanity

Abbi Kruse

In nearly 2 decades of directing early education programs, I've kept one belief central: Take good care of teachers and they will take good care of children. While that seems simple, the truth is that it is nearly impossible for most early childhood programs, which run as for-profit businesses. I've seen the effects of the business model for child care. Keeping labor costs low is the only way to create profits, but at the expense of teachers and ultimately young children. The stress level in these sites is palpable, and teachers frequently leave. Sadly, frazzled babies and children don't have that option. They don't get to resign.

For families who can afford to pay for child care what they might pay for another mortgage, there are some wonderful options. Unjustly, the children most in need of enriching early learning environments are often least likely to have access to these kinds of programs. So, in 2015, I founded the Playing Field, a nonprofit early education program aimed at minimizing disparities in early education. I wanted to create a program that any parent would choose for their own child and ensure that the program was accessible to all families.

A COMMITMENT TO CARING FOR EVERYONE

At the Playing Field, we care for children from a wide range of socioeconomic backgrounds, including children experiencing homelessness alongside those from more advantaged families. A grant from Early Head Start provides for a third of our children. Scholarship funds are available for another third, and the remaining families pay full tuition. These diverse funding sources have allowed us to build a school family that cares for children in the context of our community rather than in groups segregated by family income level.

Prioritizing the care of teachers has been the heart of our success. We know that the health and well-being of our staff is the strongest indicator of the health and well-being of our children. Adequate wages and benefits are essential. Teachers should not be forced to work second or third jobs in order to make ends meet.

Stressed teachers create stress for children. Low ratios and small group sizes are necessary. Teachers can build strong attachments and provide responsive care, *or* they can care for large numbers of children. They cannot do both. Children deserve more than assembly-line care.

Caring for staff also means equipping them with the tools needed for their very important roles. We invest heavily in training, coaching, and mentoring to support staff as they support children impacted by trauma. We are fortunate to have the financial resources to provide for our staff. However, taking care of teachers requires more than money.

As Vanessa showed us in Chapter 13, leaders have to have to understand that there is a parallel between the way we treat teachers and what they are able to offer children. Our leadership team has demonstrated the power of attuning to teachers as we ask them to attune to children. They aren't employees. They are valued members of our school family.

AND THEN COVID-19 . . .

When the pandemic hit, I had one question: How do I keep my school family safe? When the public schools in my area closed, I made the decision to close too. I understood the critical need for child care. However, my top priority had to be protecting my teachers, children, and families. If it wasn't safe for K–12 schools to meet, how could it be safe for *us*?

Along with other early educators, I was invited to participate in a call with leaders from area hospitals. Anticipating a huge impact on the medical system, they were desperate to find child care options for their essential service providers. One proposal was to put over 100 children on a racquetball court divided by bleachers. Surely no one could think that was a plausible idea. Yet the conversation continued, and I listened in stunned silence.

I surprised myself when I finally spoke up to say that I would have no part of such a plan. The levels of noise and stress would be horrible for children. In addition, I stated the obvious risk to the health of adults and children. Facing a deadly virus, and a lot of unknowns, I said we should be talking about how to care for children in smaller groups rather than larger ones. There was a brief moment of silence before the conversation continued as if I hadn't spoken.

Shortly after this, I participated in another call with our state's governor and 4,000 early educators. Most of us wanted to help our communities, but we also wanted to know how to do that safely. Masks and gloves were in short supply, meaning we could offer teachers no protection. Even diapers were hard to stock, and we didn't know if we could even function.

There were few answers and no resources offered as the governor said something like, "I have nothing to offer you, but I know you will stay open because you love children." I wanted to scream!

CHANNELING OUTRAGE INTO ACTION

The "love of children" line has long been used to silence our field whenever we dare to raise issues related to livable wages, benefits, or working conditions. Yes, we certainly do love children. And we know that children deserve better than to spend long days in large groups with exhausted teachers. These patronizing words had been spoken to us by the same person who had closed K–12 schools for the safety of their staff and children. The safety of our staff and children seemed to be of little concern.

According to research conducted at the Center for the Study of Child Care Employment, staff in early childhood care and education programs earn a national average of $11.65 per hour (McLean et al., 2021). The majority lack adequate medical benefits. Few could afford to miss work due to an extended illness. Yet the burden for assuring that our hospital systems and communities could function during a pandemic had been laid at the feet of the least resourced, lowest-paid, and most at-risk teachers. Not only were we asked to remain open to serve young children, we were asked to care for displaced school-age children as well. No one could tell me why it was unsafe for older children to be in their own schools yet safe for them to attend child care centers.

Too Good of a Plan

In response to that call, I spent hours drafting a plan that would provide 24-7 child care to emergency responders. Utilizing willing teachers from both child care and K–12 schools, we could occupy closed schools or centers to care for children in groups of 10 or fewer. Rather than opening multiple sites, I suggested we roll out openings as need demanded. I also proposed offering teachers hazard pay as well as medical coverage if they contracted COVID. I sent the plan to someone who could put it forward. It was met with enthusiasm but, I was soon informed, there were no funds for such an effort.

Conversations continued to focus on serving larger numbers of children rather than on keeping groups small. I continued to raise the issue of staff and child safety, and I continued to be dismissed. The tone seemed to be, *We need to put these kids somewhere so their parents can do important work.* My own daughters were nurses caring for COVID patients. The children they were talking about were my own grandchildren, and the teachers they were willing to risk were my own school family members. Our leaders were making decisions for the masses. It wasn't personal to them, but it was to me.

The Birth of Essential Not Expendable

Everyone was talking about how essential child care was. While I had never given much thought to the word, I began to loathe it. Essential seemed to mean we should be willing to assume the risk that K–12 teachers couldn't or wouldn't. It seemed to imply we should put our teachers (and young children) in harm's way so the lives of others could be saved. One early educator summed up my feelings when she said, "You know what is essential? Toilet paper is essential. I don't want to be treated like I'm essential. I want to be treated like I'm valuable."

Feeling helpless and exasperated, I reached out to social media. I started a Facebook group called "Essential Not Expendable." I wanted a place to recognize the importance of our work and the service we could offer to our communities while demanding that the safety of our teachers and children be prioritized. I invited my colleagues to join, and before I went to bed that evening, the group had reached 1,000 members from all around the country. It seemed I wasn't alone.

Within a year, the group grew to nearly 8,000 members. Within that space, we found others who understood the strain of navigating the unknown with little guidance and few resources. Some feared losing their businesses. Others feared exposing themselves and their families to COVID. Most feared both.

An Essential Source of Support

We faced dozens of high-stakes decisions that we felt unqualified to make. I was torn in every choice I faced. My teachers were safest at home, yet I knew they depended upon my organization for their livelihoods. I wanted to support parents and serve the families of first responders, and I knew the families who were working low-paying jobs desperately needed child care. Still, I felt the full weight of the risk to teachers, children, and parents. I had never dreamed of being in a position where my decisions literally impacted the survival of others.

On Essential Not Expendable, I not only found support, I found answers. The resources and discussions in this group helped me to develop a plan for safely reopening. A very successful strategy for us was creating outdoor classrooms. Outdoor learning had been utilized in past pandemics but was not being widely discussed. This idea, along with enhanced sanitation and safety procedures, was often posted in our group. No one told us how to operate child care during a pandemic. We figured it out together.

THE POTENTIAL POWER OF THE PROFESSION

Essential Not Expendable continues to be a place for early educators to gather and to collaborate. Our love of children motivates us to advocate for our profession—not only because we deserve better, but because children deserve better. There's a quote attributed to C. S. Lewis, "Children are not distractions from more important work. They are the most important work."

We know our work is important. We just wish others knew it as well. We cannot continue to view child care as simply a place for parents to leave their children while they go off to do important jobs. It is not a coat check service. We must recognize that the work happening in early care settings is truly the most important work and treat our early educators accordingly.

The hours a child spends in a child care setting matter. They shape who he or she will become. Early childhood teachers are far more than essential. Essential items are used while valuables are protected. It is time to value early educators and the children in their care.

REFERENCE

McLean, C., Austin, L. J. E., Whitebook, M., & Olson, K. L. (2021). *Early childhood workforce index 2020*. Center for the Study of Child Care Employment.

CHAPTER 15

Talking the Talk, Walking the Walk *With* Teachers

Lorraine Falchi and Cristina Medellin-Paz

Our process of facilitating professional learning is based upon ongoing collaborative, reflective, and humanizing conversations as essential for professional growth. This is an approach that disrupts one-size-fits-all professional learning which devalues teachers' experiences. Instead, we ground our work in a relationship-based, strength-based approach to culturally sustaining work that views teachers as capable, whole beings, worthy of sustained care.

This work provides spaces for conversations and co-reflection on the stories that shaped our lives. We often talk about our roles as mothers, women, partners, educators, and learners that have been shaped by experience and context within institutions and systems. We seek to engage teachers in recognition of their unique cultural backgrounds and personal power to critique and question educational settings. To promote conscious interaction, *we* are always cultivating our own self-awareness and examining our own biases.

In this chapter we share our work with two professionals, and as we do this, we invite you, the reader, to reflect on your experiences and relationships in educational settings, from early childhood through higher education, in order to join in a conversation that *talks back* to the ways that teachers are dehumanized in educational systems; to create more humanizing policy and practice by *walking the walk*; and to join in transforming the educational landscape.

ERIKA'S AND CRISTINA'S STORY

As an early childhood career advisor (Cristina), my role is to listen, guide, and provide support to early childhood educators. Career advisement specific to early childhood is a unique niche developed by the Early Childhood Career Development Center (ECCDC) at the New York Early

Childhood Professional Development Institute at the City University of New York (CUNY). Often students find the ECCDC because of an obstacle they are experiencing with an educational system or gatekeeping institutions (e.g., difficulties with teacher certification, international transcripts, support with college enrollment, and scholarships).

Erika is a 20-year-old Latina high school graduate who connected with the ECCDC to explore career pathways in education. During the pandemic, I was recruiting individuals to participate in an initiative that offered a fully funded credit-bearing Child Development Associate (CDA) credential. The CDA is a competency-based nationally recognized credential that prepares practitioners for the profession. I share examples of the career advisor-student relationship and how this structure served as a humanizing approach for growth.

During our first advisement session, our real work began with a conversation about exploring her motivations for wanting to pursue college and enter a profession. She began by challenging stereotypes and what goals she envisioned for herself.

> *Erika:* I don't want to be another Latina statistic, become pregnant, and not make it in life. I want to make my family proud, especially my mom. I want to go to college, but I am not sure where I should start.

As I was listening carefully to Erika's reflections, she opened up to me and shared her hopes, dreams, and aspirations, which were being confronted by stereotypes that have been perpetrated within her community of who she is supposed to be. Our advisement space was an entry point for us to develop trust through a caring relationship of compassion and humility. Her vulnerability allowed me to listen. We began to explore what career options she could imagine for herself.

Erika was a great candidate for the CDA cohort. I further began to explain the requirements of the CDA, the expectations of being a college student, and my role in this process as her career advisor. She was very humbled and excited to be part of this opportunity and was eager to begin her career as an educator.

> *Erika:* This is a great opportunity, not everyone can go to college. This is an opportunity for me to prove that I can finally do something.

During our advisement sessions, Erika reflected on how she felt in the college setting. Her self-doubt and unfamiliarity with the college system influenced how she engaged with the system. She disclosed that she had had an individualized education plan (IEP), and English was not her first language. Through our conversations, Erika had the opportunity to practice her self-advocacy skills, which empowered her to take action and seek out support for her learning. She reflected on her experience by saying, "*I felt heard and empowered to advocate for myself.*" The advisement space that we co-constructed provided an entry point for us to examine how dehumanizing experiences in schooling can have a lingering impact on how students show up in different spaces.

The relationship that Erika and I cultivated over the year grew. Erika felt safe enough to be vulnerable with me as her advisor. We developed a trusting relationship of care that allowed me as her advisor to see Erika as a whole learner and build from her strengths. Erika challenged me to explore my own biases, and I was able to be a humble learner with her.

What emerged through our conversations is a story of resilience through a culture of care. Little did I realize how impactful my role as a Latina career advisor was to Erika's journey. When Erika finished her coursework for the CDA, we spent some time reflecting on her process and journey, and I asked her, "What was your experience like?" She shared that she had experienced so many emotions going to college, especially during a pandemic. As a first-generation Latina college student with a disability, Erika confronted barriers of institutional oppression. There were many times when she wanted to just give up. She became behind in her homework as she received her job placement 6 months into the program, which impacted her ability to make meaningful connections with the course content. However, the caring relationships that she had established with her professor and with me helped her persevere. When I asked Erika to share with me what advice would she give to other students in the program, this is what she shared:

> *Erika:* Continue with what makes you happy. Don't let negative thoughts get to you. If you think negative, it won't get you anywhere. Use your self-talk to remind yourself that you can do it. Be the leader and learn to speak for yourself. It is scary that many people do not feel like they have a voice, but I want to make sure I can be a voice for others. It is important to have open communication with your professors and your career advisor. They are there to help you and listen.

Erika's voice 1 year after her participation in the CDA program with career advisement is so different from the Erika I met during our first session. Along her journey, she not only gained the required competency-based knowledge through college coursework, Erika also transformed holistically. Her determination and desire to take advantage of this opportunity to obtain her CDA became the developmental context for her transformation and growth. She knew that she had been given an opportunity, and she did not want to disappoint herself or her family and was determined to get through it. Her motivation is a powerful example that magnifies the power of relationships, especially for students of color to see people who look like them and believe in them.

MS. SPENCER'S AND LORI'S STORY

I first visited Ms. Spencer's Early Head Start program in the East New York section of Brooklyn in January 2020, and I observed her care for her children and engagement with them and families that built on 2 decades of work in her community. Baking together with her assistant teacher and their families on Pie Day, Ms. Spencer demonstrated how she cultivates a network of caring relationships with her families while weaving in her enjoyment of baking.

As a coach, I (Lori) connected with Ms. Spencer as a teacher, mother, and advocate of children and families with IEPs. Ms. Spencer decided to focus on an initial goal of conversational exchanges with her students. In our reflective conversations, Ms. Spencer was as inquisitive as one of her toddlers. She worked on extending her wait time when asking open-ended questions that stimulate language development. In mid-March 2020, in-person visits were no longer possible. We transitioned to remote teaching and learning of toddlers and remote coaching. I listened, offered affirmations of the strengths of teachers, and centered the well-being of the teachers. Thursday morning circles over Zoom began with teachers and children singing and playing instruments while Mikey, my energetic Boston terrier, jumped along with the rhythm.

Ms. Spencer sent me a text in late February 2022, prompting this exchange:

> *Hi Ms. Lori Happy Sunday. I did over my lesson plan. Well, I changed my first one. When you have time, can you tell me what you think?*

> Hi Ms. Spencer, Happy Sunday! Sure, I'd be happy to read and see.

> *Thank you, I feel like I did too much for the opening.*

> I trust you have your reasons. No problem.

In a one-on-one meeting, Ms. Spencer had decided to focus on preparing for the special education Educative Teacher Performance Assessment (edTPA), a performance-based assessment, by designing learning tasks and assessments of conceptual knowledge and skills. Teacher candidates prepare lessons and commentaries on how they organized instruction and offered children feedback in conversational exchanges, and how children respond to their feedback and instructional decisions. They submit a digital portfolio of evidence that is evaluated by external reviewers. In New York, as in the majority of states in the United States, passing edTPA helps teachers access opportunities and advance career and professional goals.

Ms. Spencer's communications about repeated revisions illustrate her concerns about edTPA-style lesson planning. In my message, I recognized her reasoning and decision-making strengths. Despite her increased self-efficacy with coaching, Ms. Spencer felt overwhelmed by not-so-authentic performance-based assessment. She was aware that this way of planning departed from her teaching practices that harnessed children's joyful investigations, curiosity, and curricular connections. Moving forward meant reconciling her work with young children and the rubrics and jargon of the edTPA. Ms. Spencer understands her context and grounds teaching and learning in her community. It is no surprise that she felt disconnected and depersonalized when working on edTPA. Her experience illuminates the full humanity of teachers who embody caring relationships among children, families, and teachers in their programs, as well as knowledge of their languages and cultures.

OUR COMMON APPROACH

We both take an inquiry stance while supporting teachers, naming and interpreting phenomena. We encourage teachers to share stories of their experiences and to encourage children's explorations and discovery. Because patterns of self-doubt and feelings of inadequacy too often plague teachers of color, we seek to understand how educational policy has sidelined research-based practices. The daily dynamics of classrooms are affected by the gatekeeping role of high-stakes assessment that impacts entry into the teaching profession. The pressure teachers internalize from navigating complex sets of institutional tasks alone is flawed. Thus, our support has included listening, guidance, and encouragement to persist despite bureaucratic, financial, and linguistic challenges. The choices they make to enact an identity that departs from stereotypes or an emergent vision of lesson planning begins with knowledge of themselves and of their children. In a parallel process, we reinforce what they can do, ask why, and help them rehearse what is challenging. In short, we provide services to unburden them, and we make the road to humanize professional relationships by walking together.

To engage in reflective inquiry, examine your "*Why?*" Think about what drew you into this profession; ask yourself, "What is my why?" A variety of motivations guide each person's path. Often in exploring why you are motivated to engage in this work, emotions surface. Each person's experiences within school systems invoke complex emotions. For individuals of color, vulnerability to microaggressions, feelings of self-doubt, a desire to be perfect, or the wounds of structural racism, gender bias, and oppression may surface within supposedly caring spaces of schools. It is important to recognize these emotions first, and listen to yourself to see how they show up in your experiences as an educator.

CREATING A CULTURE OF CARE

Teachers thrive when they feel connected and experience culturally responsive care. In reflecting on Vanessa's work, we build on her valuing teachers as curriculum developers. We agree with Abbi's stance toward nurturing her staff and organizing collective action as a part of healing. In addition, we draw on the research base that has shown the benefits of building on learners' strengths and learning from families and communities to leverage their funds of knowledge (González et al., 2005; Zentella, 2005). Too often, the cultural and linguistic knowledge and skills possessed by teachers who are bilingual and identify with the communities in which they work are dismissed. As educators, leaders and teachers humbly learn from and with communities we work with and collaboratively reflect upon assumptions, preferences, and cultural expectations when making decisions. As both Vanessa and Abbi showed us, cultivating caring educators must necessarily include reflection, critique, and action to transform unequal systems of power and privilege that many educators experience.

Through our stories, we hope to amplify the voices of two practitioners as illustrative examples of policy that is beneficial rather than harmful. We share how career advisement and coaching are powerful models of CO-reflective tools that affirm teacher identities. One-size-fits-all approaches most readily available to early childhood professionals cannot meet the diversity of teachers' needs or attend to their well-being, strengths, interests, and goals. We bring our experience walking with teachers, like Erika and Ms. Spencer, into the broader work of transforming teacher education and professional development into spaces that welcome all early childhood educators . Such practices are aligned with culturally responsive caregiving and instructional practices that have been proven to provide professional learning that is high-quality and accessible. We center humanizing experiences of caring support and recognized multidirectional relations of care between adults as rare gifts.

OUR RECOMMENDATIONS

We offer a set of recommendations to take action to mobilize with the workforce. It is imperative to recruit, retain, and grow a diverse early childhood workforce. Moving forward, we invite you to be change agents to support and expand:

- Teacher education and leadership programs designed with course sequences to engage issues of race, language, disabilities, culture, gender, and intersectional identities—for both children and adults;
- Professional learning models (coaching, training, advising) with an image of the educator as a competent, whole person;
- Ongoing investment higher education spaces as developmental settings that invite adult learning that builds reflective capacity and fosters an inquiry stance and culturally responsive practices in parallel processes with instructors, colleagues, and professional development supporters;
- Program and curriculum design be critically examined, evaluated, and grounded in intentional teaching and culturally responsive frameworks that honor and affirm positive social identities (race, language, culture, religion, gender identity and expression, disabilities, etc.); and
- Pedagogical approaches that draw on collaborative creation of meaningful learning experiences; develop identities; promote intellectual growth, moral development, and the capacity to reason; recognize and critique societal inequalities; and solve real-world problems.

REFERENCES

González, N., Moll, L. C., & Amanti, C. (2005). *Funds of knowledge*. Lawrence Erlbaum.

Zentella, A. C. (2005). Premises, promises, and pitfalls of language socialization research in Latino families and communities. In A. C. Zentella (Ed.), *Building on strength* (pp. 13–30). Teachers College Press.

Part VI

WHOSE STANDARDS?

Standardization has long been (re)shaping early years curriculum and assessment, and its ripple effect has impacted care and education for young children and adults alike. Stephanie Curenton and Alexandra Figueras-Daniel's essay provides a sociopolitical-historical overview of standardization and its impact on early childhood programs, situating the landscape of standardization through a lens of race and language. Using reflection and vision-oriented framing, they share ways in which standards, curriculum, and assessment can be more expansive and inclusive. Margarita Ruiz Guerrero and Carolyn Brennan invite readers to engage with their work in teacher education, bringing attention to the problems inherent in settler-colonial approaches to early childhood. They highlight a specific NAEYC Professional Development Standard to show what is possible when working with the both/and or when meeting/challenging regulatory forces. Further, their essay amplifies the adoption of aesthetic approaches that "truly honor the lives and experiences of the community we serve." Evandra Catherine shares recommendations around standards, curriculum, and assessment and how they can be more inclusive and expansive toward race, language, culture, disability, and neurodiversity.

CHAPTER 16

Being Held to *Whose* Standards?

Considering the Unique Experiences of Racially and Ethnically Diverse Children

Alexandra Figueras-Daniel and Stephanie M. Curenton

By its very nature, the word "standards" implies sameness. Literally, in *Webster's Dictionary*, the word is defined as "a level of quality, achievement, especially one that people generally consider normal or acceptable." The question in the early years is: What is considered "normal," and who were these expectations based upon? Further, in adopting standards that are not necessarily based on the strengths of all children, how, then, can curriculum and assessment adequately serve diverse children on a day-to-day basis? Although standards have attempted to move the United States toward educational *equality*, in this chapter we ponder how a traditional education standards framework can be modified to make learning goals and expectations more *equitable* for children who are racially, linguistically, and ethnically diverse. In thinking about this question, it is helpful to reflect on how we got here and who was at the table when the notion of education standards was conceptualized and subsequently modified as time has gone on.

HISTORICAL REFLECTION ON STANDARDS-BASED REFORM THROUGH THE LENS OF RACE AND LANGUAGE

The first federal education legislation, the Elementary and Secondary Education Act of 1965, was part of President Johnson's War on Poverty and was further catalyzed by the Reagan administration's report *A Nation at Risk* (National Commission on Excellence in Education, 1983). Since that time, educational innovations and reforms have been implemented in a variety of ways and alongside a multitude of educational programs to increase children's academic performance. The common denominator of all, however, has been the obvious: to "fix" low-achieving, synonymously minority, children. Extending this, however, it is also true that the standards that we have come to know today have been and continue to be based on majority-white populations, forever indebting students of color to a set of norms and practices not structured to highlight their strengths, but rather that have created curricula and assessments that constrain rather than develop intellectualism. Further, the standards-based reform instituted high-stakes accountability assessments that consistently overlook harder-to-measure skills (like oral language, broad cultural knowledge, other languages, etc.).

Standards-based reform, born under the Clinton administration in the 1994 reauthorization of the Elementary and Secondary Education Act (ESEA), gave way to the highest accountability provisions for states and school districts through the No Child Left Behind Act, the Bush administration's seventh authorization of the law in 2001. These laws not only gave way to standards, but also to their accompanying pieces, assessment and curriculum that could adequately cover the content outlined by the standards. Further, accountability for teachers including the measurement of teacher practices through rubrics and frameworks was also added to the accountability formulas. Additionally, the movement also gave rise to standards-based report cards, aiming to focus on what children know and can do in connection with standards and to lessen the subjectivity of grading for teachers and parents and generally in effort to make grades fairer. Despite the well-intentioned effort, however, one could argue that these report cards further alienate parents who don't always have clear understandings of how their children are being graded and what the numbers represent about their growth. For speakers of languages other than English, it could further be assumed that these report cards do not support supportive school-home connections.

In 1995, Diane Ravitch, then a strong advocate for standards, laid out all the critiques that she foresaw against the use of standards. In conclusion, she articulated that "If the act of setting standards is seen as the first step in educational reform, rather than the end of the process, then standards can become a means of ensuring equality of opportunity" (p. 22). Twenty-seven years and four reauthorizations of federal educational legislation later, we question if standards have been able to accomplish what they set out to do. Despite the fact that Ravitch has recanted many of her educational opinions, one thing remains true: the appendages of standards-based reform are alive and well, despite evidence that the achievement gap persists. If we were to continue along Ravitch's initial line of thinking, now is the perfect time to think about the next step.

UNMASKING THE POLITICAL DIVIDE: NATIONAL
STANDARDS FROM THE LENS OF POLITICS

More recently, standards were again part of political conversations in the age of the Common Core beginning in 2009, in which state governors and state-level education officials collaborated to develop a set of standards to be adopted by states in hopes of creating more consistent goals from state to state, with a total of 41 states, the District of Columbia, four territories, and the Department of Defense Education Activity (DoDEA) eventually adopting the standards. Despite that at the time politicians argued against the idea of the Common Core, and there were widespread misunderstandings about what the Common Core was, it was clear that states of both political affiliations subscribed to the idea. Further, given that the effort was not led by any federal players, it seemed more bipartisan in its conception. Additionally, the collaboration called upon teachers and the public to provide feedback on the standards as they were developed. Consequently, it is clear that the political debate around standards is actually an artificial one that has simply been used as a divisive tool, when in actuality the need for national standards is something that most current-day liberals and pre-populist conservatives believed in (Whitman, 2015).

Surprisingly, after the Obama administration's great push and successful state take-up of the Common Core standards, the reauthorization of the Elementary and Secondary Education Act in 2015, known as the Every Student Succeeds Act (ESSA), which was passed just as President Obama left office, did not actually have any requirement that states continue to adopt the Common Core Standards, even if they had already agreed to them. Perhaps this was a concession in order to get the current Republicans to sign on to the bill, and if so, it worked because ESSA passed with bipartisan support. Thus, even after the long political battle over national standards that has been waging since the Reagan administration and that has crossed over from a Republican issue to a Democratic issue, society now sits in our present day of 2022 with no national standards—the Common Core standards are dead, and instead we are back to state-specific standards.

STANDARDS VARIABILITY FROM STATE TO STATE AND
IMPLICATIONS FOR DIVERSE LEARNERS

At the heart of the matter, the reason national standards became an issue that, at one point, both political parties supported is because of the desire for all children across the United States to be expected to be learning the same skills at the same developmental stages. This rationale makes sense given the wide variety in how education is implemented across the nation. Education is a right that is granted at the state level, and as a result, states have great autonomy in determining what children learn, how they are taught, and how they are assessed. Such variation results in different expectations, across states and U.S. territories, for children's achievement across the grades as to at what time children are supposed to learn what. This creates a problem for our national population because educators cannot be certain that a child in one state has the same knowledge as a child from another state, which is problematic given the high rate of interstate mobility among families with children. Thus, most policymakers in both aisles can see the rational need for national standards because such standards allow us as a nation to know *what* children at each grade should know and be able to do.

Ultimately, the crux of the disagreement stems from *how* these standards are taught through implementation of curriculum, and the assessments used to measure how children are progressing toward the standards. All of this is particularly related to the content and *how* these standards are assessed, especially in terms of when (and how frequently) children are tested, who is tested, and what mode of assessment is used. As an example, in thinking about content, it is easy to see how a state like Texas might support the teaching of historical content that may look very different from that of Massachusetts. This could be particularly disempowering to racially diverse students, who may be more demographically present in one state versus another. Further, in thinking about assessment, how we select assessments appropriately has even deeper implications, as invalid tests that are not appropriately normed for a particular population also matters in allowing children to be seen in equitable ways.

WHERE DO WE GO FROM HERE?

Despite political divides and ever-changing standards-based reforms, there is evidence that should not be discounted that use of standards has improved educational outcomes (as traditionally measured) over the past 25 years, but gaps still persist (Hansen et al., 2018). In thinking about educational innovations such as child-directed instructional approaches, Pre-K–3 alignments, school calendar changes, and so forth that have promising findings, it seems that many education reformers have spent 40 years focused on many of the wrong things.

In the book *Segregation by Experience,* Jennifer Adair and Kiyomi Sánchez-Suzuki Colegrove (2021) explore the opportunity for agency in elementary classrooms. Through an ethnographic study, they document children's agency in a 1st-grade classroom through video, which they show to teachers, children, and parents to get their reactions to what they saw. Their findings are fascinating, as they document a variety of reactions from each group. In perhaps the most striking example, a group of teachers become visibly frustrated and upset, citing their frustration at never being able to lead classrooms where children can have agency due to constraints placed by their district, which include strict pacing guides and time schedules that they must always follow.

Given our work in many large, diverse school districts, these reactions hit home. We have heard this from teachers and witnessed it in our observations of classrooms time and time again: frustrated teachers who realize that they are not treated professionally, who are not given the deference of being the most knowledgeable about their students and their individualized needs as learners and being tightly constrained by the district/ programmatic-imposed practices aimed at standards fidelity. In our experience, teachers particularly frustrated with this are those who work with English learners, who would obviously have trouble sticking to the pacing guide of all the others as children struggle not only to learn a new language, but to keep up academically with concepts presented in a foreign language.

In reflecting on this finding from Adair and Sánchez-Suzuki Colegrove's book, we wonder not whether standards are needed, but rather, *How can we better leverage standards to teach the populations we are most concerned with?* And *how can we better apply an assets-focused framework to assessment and curriculum?* Going back to *Webster's* definition of standard we presented in our chapter's introduction, these questions lead us to ask that if children of color are not being given sufficient time to learn content and a new language, is this really an acceptable "level of quality"? Further, what are the measures used to keep schools accountable to these truths?

One thing is clear: We don't suggest throwing standards away, and also do not espouse the idea that teachers be able to change state standards on their own. On the contrary, we would like to suggest below a set of ideas that can provide supports for advocacy that can be enacted by teachers and school-level leaders to think more equitably about children and families from diverse backgrounds, along with the ways in which standards, assessments, and curriculum are implemented in schools every day:

1. Add depth to standards by drawing on students' rich cultural and racial backgrounds to create responsive environments and develop children's identities. Gholdy Muhammad (2020) suggests that teaching must explicitly build on and cultivate students' identities. Though curriculum that aligns with standards is typical, the question becomes who can support the editing of curriculum to accomplish this. From our standpoint, educational leaders and work groups that include teachers to think carefully about lessons and texts that add this dimension to every content standard are necessary.

2. Rethink the idea of developmentally appropriate practice in early elementary schools. We know for a fact that elementary schools adhere to rigid schedules and pacing guides, which do little to offer children opportunities to make decisions about their learning, peer groupings, and so on (Ritchie & Gutmann, 2013). In New Jersey, for example, although Race to the Top funds were utilized by the New Jersey Department of Education (2015) to establish cutting-edge *First Through Third Grade Implementation Guidelines* that attempted to implement these kinds of approaches, very little traction occurred, despite a state effort to grant training to teachers to learn and implement the guidelines.

3. Recruit, develop, and retain a cadre of BIPOC teachers/teacher leaders who are well versed in culturally and linguistically responsive practices to translate standards and be the authority. These groups can best meet the needs of their communities and can provide insights about curriculum as related to the development of cultural and linguistic identities.

4. Curate and offer professional development experiences to teachers and systems that align well to these ideas. While there is clearly a mismatch between current school/education leaders and the communities they serve, there must be ways of guiding leaders to select professional development (PD) that is meaningful for this purpose. Moreover, training that extends beyond one day or checkbox approaches to satisfying cursory needs is necessary to do this. Included in this should be opportunities for families to weigh in on what they perceive as needs to be addressed by the teachers working with their children.

5. Create a pipeline of BIPOC teachers who can aspire to positions of leadership who both understand issues of equity from a personal place but are also equipped with the knowledge and expertise needed to advocate for children and families through choice of curriculum, assessments, and so on.

6. Re-examine the constructs that we are valuing in the current assessment of children and think about what strengths are being left out.

7. Create a systematic effort to use assessment data in meaningful ways that align standards with cultural and linguistic diversities, families, and teacher observation data.

8. Consider the use of classroom observation measures that explicitly look at the ways in which diverse children experience the classroom as well as the ways in which teachers are given feedback and how they are supported to improve.

9. Strive to better prepare teachers to understand the importance of cultural and linguistic responsiveness and the need to develop children's identities.

REFERENCES

Adair, J., & Sánchez-Suzuki Colegrove, K. (2021). *Segregation by experience.* University of Chicago Press.

Hansen, M., Mann Levesque, E., Quintero, D., & Valant, J. (2018). *Have we made progress on achievement gaps?* https://www.brookings.edu/blog/brown-center-chalkboard/2018/04/17/have-we-made-progress-on-achievement-gaps-looking-at-evidence-from-the-new-naep-results/

Muhammad, G. (2020). *Cultivating genius: An equity framework for culturally and historically responsive literacy.* Scholastic.

National Commission on Excellence in Education. (1983). *A nation at risk: The imperative for educational reform.*

New Jersey Department of Education. (2015). *First through third grade implementation guidelines.*

Ravitch, D. (1995). *National standards in American education: A citizen's guide.* Brookings Institution Press.

Ritchie, S., & Gutmann, L. (Eds.). (2013). *FirstSchool: Transforming PreK-3rd-grade education for African American, Latino, and low-income children.* Teachers College Press.

Whitman, D. (2015). *The surprising roots of the Common Core.* Brookings Institute, Brown Center on Education Policy.

CHAPTER 17

Using Aesthetic Approaches to Meet and Challenge the National Standards

A Both/And Approach

Margarita G. Ruiz Guerrero and Carolyn Brennan

OUR INDIVIDUAL JOURNEYS

When I (Margarita) studied for my master's in early childhood education, the literature was similar to what I previously learned in nutrition, emphasizing the importance of the stages of child development, National Association for the Education of Young Children (NAEYC), and identifying early signs for intervention. When addressing parent and family involvement in both education and nutrition, the purpose was to "educate" them.

Later, as a doctoral student, I was introduced to feminisms of color and critical perspectives that challenged me so much that at first I resisted them. As I further engaged with these readings, however, I began to realize I was part of the machinery of perpetuating normalized ideas and power dynamics. These normalized ideas oversimplify the "problem" by blaming parents for what I (the professional) assumed was a lack of care toward their children. That first class shook my identity as a "professional." My analysis of this well-organized machinery and my emerging understanding of inequity changed my way of being. Now, as a Mexican-Latina scholar working in the United States, my work focuses on unearthing complex power dynamics, identity intersections, and systematic oppression.

Like Margarita, my (Carolyn) previous experiences have shaped my current work. As a graduate student teaching at the university level for the first time, I naively imagined myself packing tool kits with strategies for my students, who would then partner with families. Before long, I realized I was actually fueling their steamrollers, as these burgeoning professionals used their newly found "expertise" to identify what families were doing wrong. Assignments and class discussions were peppered with concerning comments: "This family does not care about education." "What do I do if parents don't want to do the right thing?"

These questions ultimately fueled an examination of my courses and the intersection of my teaching and my identities, particularly those that hold dominant power (I am white, cisgendered, straight, and able-bodied). I sought out methods for helping students see the role of power in school–family relationships. Years later I had a watershed moment when a colleague sent me an article about the use of Black feminist photovoice (Pérez et al., 2016), an approach where research participants take photographs of, and narrate, what is meaningful in their lives (see Pérez et al., 2016, for further description). I read the article while traveling for a job interview and soon learned that one of the authors, Margarita, had also accepted a position in the same program. This has given me the opportunity to learn from and with my colleague as we navigate teaching in a nationally accredited program that is dedicated to social justice.

OUR WORK TOGETHER

As teacher educators, we hope that our courses will provide supportive opportunities for student transformations similar to the ones we have experienced over our academic careers. We take this journey together in a course on families and community relationships in early childhood education that Margarita teaches on the main campus and Carolyn on a secondary campus. Our students are encouraged to question their educational journeys and explore what is taught in schools and whose histories and perspectives have been left out.

Students discuss the impact of systemic injustice on the lives of children and families from diverse backgrounds and come to understand their own identities in relationship to power, privilege, and the experiences that have shaped their ways of thinking and being. To do this, we are guided by Black feminist theories and decolonizing frameworks that urge us to consider multiple knowledges and maintain a constant critical self-reflection. Based on Margarita's previous work (Pérez et al., 2016), we use Black feminist photovoice as a tool for this exploration and now add decolonizing frameworks in our analysis to support our students' (and our own) understanding of multiple knowledges and the spaces we inhabit. We offer this work acknowledging that we do not hold all the knowledge, nor is this the only way possible.

BOTH/AND: MEETING AND CHALLENGING
THE NATIONAL STANDARDS

Standards in ECE are a policy response to the widely disparate experiences children have in early learning settings (and life in general). We understand the intended benefits of these documents but worry about pitfalls and hidden agendas that come with standardization, a tool that reifies settler-colonial approaches to education. For example, our course is aligned with NAEYC's *Professional Standards and Competencies for Early Childhood Educators* (2019): Standard 2, "Family-teacher partnerships and community connections." Among other expectations, this standard encourages teachers to actively cultivate respectful and reciprocal relationships with families. We agree with this idea but note that while the document provides sound reasoning for creating relationships, it omits any discussion of the historic and ongoing inequitable power dynamics and the impact of settler-colonial constructs of schooling on teacher–family relationships. In the absence of this context, teachers are likely to not only make troubling assumptions about families but engage in interactions that maintain unequal power dynamics.

We use Black feminist photovoice assignments to help students build their knowledge where the standards leave off. Students capture abstract images of Patricia Hill Collins's (2000) Domains of Power (see Figure 17.1) and use them to express their own understandings of the marginalization of specific minoritized identities (e.g., Indigenous, LGBTQ+, etc.) and reflect on how they will end cycles of oppression in their own work with children and families.

Symbolic representation, a cornerstone of the assignment, reflects the perspectives of scholars, particularly women of color (e.g., hooks, 1994; Lorde, 1984), who argue that breaking down traditional systems of power requires space for creative expression, like Black feminist photovoice. In the example below (Figure 17.2), we show how this assignment created an opportunity for a student, Alma, to explore hegemonic power and Indigenous resilience:

> This is a picture of what used to be a railroad track a long time ago. I took this picture at the Whatcom Falls Park in Bellingham, Washington. As you can see, there are trees all around the track, but there is also moss growing on it. I wanted to take this photo because to me it represents how not just Native Americans, but also everyone can *grow and become resilient even when they are faced with difficult obstacles*. If you think of the moss being the Lummi nation and the track being the laws enforced by the white men, it shows how the Lummi nation can grow from this.

The imagery in the photo and the text bring to mind notions of past and present that beautifully reflect her understanding of the oppressive realities of Indigenous peoples whose experiences are framed in the dominant culture as relics of the past, yet whose struggle and resilience are ever-present, as has been discussed by Native scholars (Tuck & Yang, 2012). In this image, Alma demonstrates her understanding of both

Figure 17.1. Patricia Hill Collins's Domains of Power

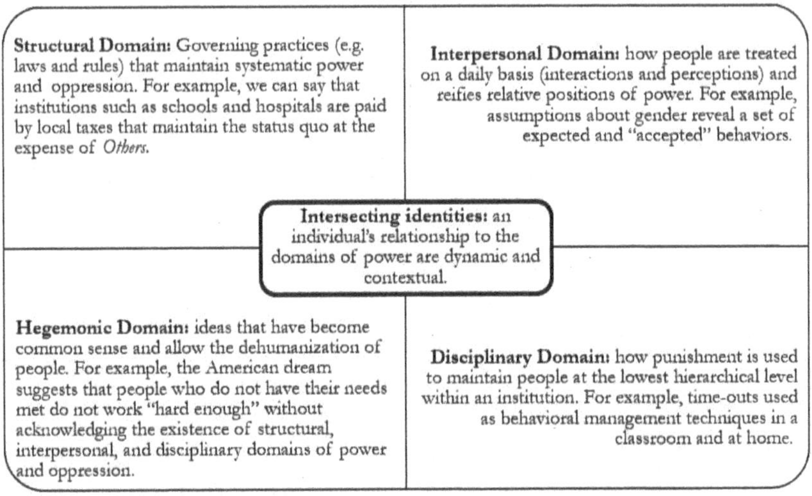

Structural Domain: Governing practices (e.g. laws and rules) that maintain systematic power and oppression. For example, we can say that institutions such as schools and hospitals are paid by local taxes that maintain the status quo at the expense of *Others*.

Interpersonal Domain: how people are treated on a daily basis (interactions and perceptions) and reifies relative positions of power. For example, assumptions about gender reveal a set of expected and "accepted" behaviors.

Intersecting identities: an individual's relationship to the domains of power are dynamic and contextual.

Hegemonic Domain: ideas that have become common sense and allow the dehumanization of people. For example, the American dream suggests that people who do not have their needs met do not work "hard enough" without acknowledging the existence of structural, interpersonal, and disciplinary domains of power and oppression.

Disciplinary Domain: how punishment is used to maintain people at the lowest hierarchical level within an institution. For example, time-outs used as behavioral management techniques in a classroom and at home.

Figure 17.2. Railroad Tracks, Whatcom Falls Park

historic and current realities. Her language is reflective of her new relationship with critical thinking related to resiliency. She is trying on ideas but still has more to learn. We don't think she believes that the Lummi nation grows from these laws, but rather in spite of them. While she begins to play with these ideas, we believe that the centering of *Others'*, in this case Indigenous people's, existent realities is a necessary step in the creation of community partnerships as required in NAEYC Standard 2. Doing so allows us to more authentically enter into partnerships, as we can more clearly see how a history of oppression may impact the ways in which individuals interact with others. This work also has the potential to shape our collective consciousness and encourage us to question and resist hegemonic/normalized dominance, and finally generate possibilities of change.

> For example, *the Lummi are taking a stand against the largest coal export in the country*. They are taking a stand because this terminal will destroy their fishing grounds. They have a lot of companies working against them, "But the Lummis have a power of their own: They are a sovereign nation within the United States, a self-governing community with control over their land and water" (Treaty Rights and Totem Poles, 2015). Because the Lummi have their own government, they are in control of their land and water and no one else is.

Here Alma continues to explore the intersection of systemic oppression and resiliency. Her comments expose a central point of conflict, they are in control of their land and water and no one else is, and yet the Lummi people have to stand up against the U.S. government and a powerful coal industry. The treaties exist, and yet they will not be honored without a fight. This tension exists not only for the Lummi nation, but is reflected in settler-colonialism in all its forms. We are reminded of the NAEYC standards, another document filled with promise that ultimately falls flat unless we work to understand the context within which school–family relationships exist.

> This is related to the actions I will take to break the cycle of oppression by standing up for what is right and helping those in need. For example, if a family is being affected by certain actions from white men or laws, I will help them look for resources and find the right people to talk to so they can get help.

Standards prioritize specific bodies of research, ways of being, and preferred child outcomes that reflect the norms of the dominant culture (e.g., white, high socioeconomic status, able-bodied) while reinforcing dominant cultural narratives about children, families, the role of education, and family–school partnerships. In this excerpt, Alma is conscious that by centering the lived experiences, problematizing the existent realities, and deeply analyzing historic events, she can improve her relationships with families and ultimately act as a partner in resisting oppression.

While there is work to be done troubling her notions of who is "in need," Alma is beginning to see that identities are related to power and oppression and that this reality must be part of her interactions in schools. We suggest that this awareness can prevent the more common teacher–family disconnections and detachment that are steeped in preconceived ideas of professionals as knowledgeable and parents as ignorant or uncaring. When students understand the role of history and systemic injustice, they can begin to recognize where their notions of superiority as professionals originate and perhaps shift their ways of being with families.

They also develop a fuller understanding of, and respect for, the resilience and strength of the communities with whom they work that is often in contrast to the narrative they have been previously fed through schooling and the media. Awareness of the context that surrounds families may have a positive impact on this student's expectations when entering into relationships, given their relative power in school settings compared to families. We suggest that teachers' and students' mindfulness and self-reflection will guide them to embrace an emphatic, holistic approach toward children and their families that values their knowledges and ways of being.

Using aesthetic approaches such as photovoice, we reach the intended goal of the NAEYC standard. However, we use a perspective that truly honors the lives and experiences of the community we serve. This is an example of how students foster a reciprocal learning experience and build community collaborations knowing the importance of coalition and combined actions that exist among children, families, and teachers.

DISCUSSION

This chapter is an example of how early years teacher preparation programs can simultaneously meet national professional preparation standards while supporting students in broadening their understanding of systemic oppression and its impact on education. In a world where critical race theory is under attack, teacher candidates require a space where they can use multiple languages and ways of thinking to explore their understanding of power and oppression and their own role in these systems. While we have used Black feminist photovoice and decolonizing frameworks to broaden students' understanding of family engagement, we believe this approach can also be used to help students understand a wide range of topics and current events that impact very young children and families, including current immigration policies, the Black Lives Matter movement, and others. We offer this piece being aware that we, as Saavedra and Pérez (2012) point out, "must continue to learn language from, and create new language for, our theoretical spaces that help us to express and navigate the complexity and multiple locations of struggles and resistance" (p. 430). Decolonizing frameworks and thinking are tasks that require constant reflection, constant rethinking, and constant reimagining of new ways of being, teaching, and learning. These constant reflections—praxis and reflexivity—push us to question everything, which we find a very hard yet inspiring thing to do.

REFERENCES

Collins, P. H. (2000). *Black feminist thought*. Routledge.

hooks, b. (1994). *Teaching to transgress*. Routledge.

Lorde, A. (1984). *Sister outsider*. The Crossing Press.

National Association for the Education of Young Children (NAEYC). (2019). *Professional standards and competencies for early childhood educators*.

Pérez, M. S., Ruiz Guerrero, M. G., & Mora, E. (2016). Black feminist photovoice. *Journal of Early Childhood Teacher Education, 37*(1), 41–60.

Saavedra, C. M., & Pérez, M. S. (2012). Chicana and Black feminisms. *Equity and Excellence in Education, 45*(3), 430–443.

Tuck, E., & Yang, K. W. (2012). Decolonization is not a metaphor. *Decolonization: Indigeneity, Education & Society, 1*(1), 1–40.

Treaty Rights and Totem Poles. (2015, February 13). http://exp.grist.org/lumm

CHAPTER 18

"John Adams Didn't Own Slaves"

Culturally Affirming Standards, Assessments, and Curriculum

Evandra Catherine

> The objective of this assessment is not to make saintly men out of the presidents, but to acknowledge their accomplishments . . . framed within their proper context.
>
> —Ma'asehyahu Isra-Ul, *Richmond Times-Dispatch,* March 20, 2022

My son is in the 6th grade and attends public school. He recently came home and shared that his school would be offering a performance-based assessment (PBA) in lieu of the history/social science standards of learning (SOLs). In 2015, the Virginia Department of Education released guidance that local districts can use state-developed performance tasks (e.g., PBAs) to confer locally awarded verified credits in history and social science. Due to COVID's impact on teaching, many school districts in Virginia are offering PBAs. One of the state's history standards, which covers the timeframe of the 1770s to the early 1800s, specifically states, "students will apply social science skills to understand the challenges faced by the new nation by describing the major accomplishments of the first five presidents of the United States (USI.7c)" (Board of Education, Commonwealth of Virginia, 2008, p. 23).

To demonstrate understanding of this standard, students are required to create a memorial or monument to one of the first five presidents. This assessment was troubling for several reasons, including the retraumatization I experienced associated with this history and having to talk to my 11-year-old about it. Second, as a Black parent, I do not want my son to be taught to memorialize the individuals responsible for the social and economic positions of many Blacks today, especially without proper framing and context. Last, beyond my personal feelings, my son's response to the assignment added to the trauma of it all. He says, "Well, John Adams didn't own slaves, I could do it [the assessment] on him."

I asked my son's teacher if he could memorialize Toussaint L'Ouverture instead, since he was responsible for Haiti's independence, which led to that nation's abolition of slavery in 1805. I felt this history was more appropriate for my Black son, because it was (a) occurring at the same time as the founding of the United States and (b) directly related to his lived experience. His teacher responded with, "I didn't develop the assessment; it was developed by the district." This response left me frustrated because as a parent, I could not request a change in assessment for my child because (a) the assessment was developed by the district and not the teacher, and (b) the standard being assessed was established by the state.

Feeling unsettled, I reached out to the district's history specialist, whose response was, "The objective of this assessment is not to make saintly men out of the presidents, but to acknowledge their accomplishments . . . framed within their proper context." He immediately changed the language of the assessment, stating that "in Virginia we need history without hagiography," yet he had no power to change the state standard (in Williams, 2022, para. 12). This experience demonstrates the need for this series and a deeper understanding of the experiences of culturally diverse children and families with state standards, assessments, and curriculum. Furthermore, I share this experience because a place where policymakers have been successfully perpetuating false narratives has been in state standards and assessments.

At the opening of this section, Alex and Stephanie describe how states have autonomy to determine how children are assessed. Thus, it is not surprising that Virginia's state leaders would place emphasis on the accomplishments of the first five presidents, four of which were from Virginia. Unfortunately for racially, ethnically, and linguistically diverse children, standards lead to biased assessments and curriculum. This is especially the case when teaching history. Teachers are forced to teach history as if it is linear, as opposed to connecting U.S. history to the history of Africans and other Indigenous peoples during this time frame.

There is undoubtedly an increased amount of harm associated with biased standards, assessments, and curricula for culturally diverse children and their families, and others. Unfortunately, schools are neither prepared nor have the internal supports needed to repair these harms. In Chapter 17, Ruiz Guerrero and Brennan discuss the importance of using aesthetic approaches to meet challenging standards, especially as we navigate history as told from the perspective of the colonizer. The next sections briefly summarize the evidence on early learning standards, assessments, and curriculum and provide suggestions for ensuring that stakeholders consider equity and inclusion in these key issue areas.

STANDARDS

Early childhood learning and education in the United States is fragmented and thus guided by standards developed by various federal and state agencies and professional organizations. Because of this, the quality of standards depends greatly on the program and funding mechanism. For example, in Head Start, a popular federal early childhood program, standards were updated during President Obama's administration to include key equity provisions. They prohibit the use of harsh discipline (e.g., suspension, expulsion, corporal punishment), which disproportionately affects racially, ethnically, and linguistically diverse children; require programs to provide bilingual learning for bilinguals/multilinguals when a portion of the children in a program speak the same home language; and include children with disabilities throughout the standards.

Unfortunately, Head Start programs reach only a very small percentage of the nation's early childhood population. To fill in the gap, most states have developed early learning programs primarily for 4-year-olds and children with disabilities from birth to age 5. State early learning standards are designed to define expectations for children's learning and development prior to kindergarten entry and are in essence a reflection of how states conceptualize children's readiness for school. Similar to K–12 state standards, the evidence indicates that state early learning standards usually reflect the views of the persons involved in their development, and in some cases may not be aligned with the research on children's early learning and development (Scott-Little et al., 2006.)

Also, early learning standards include very few equity provisions, specifically around the use of discipline and inclusion of children with disabilities in settings with their peers without disabilities. This is problematic, particularly for children with disabilities; since they are guaranteed the right to a free appropriate public education, they are often served across all early childhood programs. This has implications for a national set of standards, especially for these children. Thus, to address these omissions and variations across programs, federal agencies have released recommendations to states that ensure that all state and local early learning programs consider the discipline and inclusion of young children.

These efforts by federal agencies (U.S. Departments of Education and Health and Human Services, 2015), along with the updated Head Start standards, show a greater level of focus on issues of equity in early childhood at the federal level compared to states' focus. This in part could largely be due to civil rights monitoring of inequities in key areas such as discipline of culturally diverse children and children with disabilities, and the inclusion of children with disabilities in settings with their peers. Additionally, with the exception of Head Start standards, most state early learning standards promote the use of universal and able-bodied curriculum as opposed to inclusive and culturally responsive approaches such as (a) universal design for learning, (b) trauma-informed approaches, (c) strengths-based curriculum, (d) translanguaging, and (e) the use of settings that implement natural proportions of children with and without disabilities.

Last, in addition to learning standards, professional organizations such as the National Association for the Education of Young Children (NAEYC) and the Council for Exceptional Children (CEC) have developed standards to professionalize the early childhood field, guide teacher preparation and training, and highlight the use of developmentally appropriate practices for all children. While there have been some shifts in mindsets of early childhood professional organizations over the years (e.g., NAEYC & CEC's Developmentally Appropriate Practices and equity statements), efforts fall short of being culturally affirming or understanding development in the context of racially, ethnically, and linguistically diverse environments.

In addition to Figueras-Daniel and Curenton's next steps for thinking more equitably about children and families from diverse backgrounds, I will reference a resource that I co-authored that outlines a process for developing equitable and universal standards that support every child. Given the comprehensive nature, proven success, and equity provisions included in the Head Start standards, my co-authors and I, at the Children's Equity Project, released a brief titled *Building a Universal Preschool System Around Head Start* that describes how Head Start standards have improved programs' overall quality of services and key equity provisions (Meek et al., 2021). Key provisions include restrictions or prohibitions on discipline and requirements that programs provide bilingual learning for dual-language learners, and that children with disabilities are fully included in all program services and activities.

While the field may be a long way from a universal early learning system, states can review their early learning standards and better align them with Head Start standards, particularly around equitable considerations. Also, professional organizations can better align their equity efforts around professionalization, teaching, and learning with Head Start standards. By considering equity in early learning standards, programs can design assessments and curriculum that more accurately reflect the skills and abilities of culturally diverse children. Below, I will briefly summarize the literature on assessments and curriculum in early learning and offer equitable suggestions for success with culturally diverse children.

ASSESSMENT AND CURRICULUM

Assessments and curriculum (Grisham-Brown et al., 2006) in early childhood learning are largely driven by federal and state standards. The literature reveals that early childhood assessments provide valuable information on individual children's learning and development across the essential domains of school readiness. A common assessment used across states is a kindergarten entry assessment (KEA). KEAs are administered within a few months of kindergarten entry and have been promoted as having the potential to mitigate gaps in early learning and development.

Unfortunately, these assessments are highly subjective (based on teacher report), are often misaligned with preschool assessments, and emphasize certain skills over others. With a growing reliance on teachers as assessors of children's performance, questions have been raised about how accurately teachers' judgments reflect children's performance and school readiness. For example, the evidence indicates that kindergarten teachers' assessments of children at entry are more valid than preschool teachers' assessment of children exiting preschool.

Also problematic is the use of norm-referenced and universal screenings with children with disabilities. According to the Early Childhood Technical Assistance center's website, states use several different assessments and approaches to measure children with disabilities' functional and social emotional skills (SEL). While most states use a process that includes information from various sources, there is great subjectivity within the team. Moreover, states report these data in aggregate form, limiting the field's understanding of the experiences of children with disabilities who have been racialized. In fact, most data from standardized assessments in early childhood are often in aggregate form, do not account for children's intersecting identities, and are not aligned with widely used curriculum (e.g., High Scope, Second Step, Creative Curriculum).

Last, early childhood curriculum varies widely. Some curricula target academic skills, while others target social-emotional skills. Often, these two types of curriculum are not integrated, meaning that most programs use academic curricula supported by the use of a social emotional learning curricula such as PATHS or Incredible Years. Nonetheless, the primary goal of early learning curriculum is to promote learning and development in social, emotional, and cognitive domains. Unfortunately, similar to the literature on assessments and standards, the field relies on curricula that are absent of the lived experiences and ways of knowing of culturally diverse children, bilinguals, and children with disabilities.

As Ruiz Guerrero and Brennan wrote in the previous chapter, "decolonizing frameworks and thinking are tasks that require constant reflection, constant rethinking, and constant reimagining of new ways of being, teaching, and learning." As the field considers the development of equity-focused early learning curricula, there has to be an intentional effort to incorporate the rich histories and lived experiences of culturally diverse children and families, and curricula must value the funds of knowledge that culturally diverse children and families bring to early learning environments. Further, the field must rely on the research of scholars of colors and adopt curricula that allow for accurately assessing the strengths of culturally diverse children.

REFERENCES

Board of Education, Commonwealth of Virginia. (2008). *History and social science standards of learning curriculum framework 2008.*

Grisham-Brown, J., Hallam, R., & Brookshire, R. (2006). Using authentic assessment to evidence children's progress toward early learning standards. *Early Childhood Education Journal, 34*(1), 45–51.

Meek, S., Williams, C., Bostic, B., Iruka, I.U., Blevins, D., Catherine, E., & Alexander, B. (2021). *Building a universal system around Head Start.* Children's Equity Project.

Scott-Little, C., Kagan, S. L., & Frelow, V. S. (2006). Conceptualization of readiness and the content of early learning standards: The intersection of policy and research? *Early Childhood Research Quarterly, 21*(2), 153–173.

United States Department of Education, & United States Department of Health and Human Services. (2015, September 14). *Policy statement on inclusion of children with disabilities in early childhood programs.* https://www2.ed.gov/about/inits/ed/earlylearning/inclusion/index.html

Williams, M. P. (2022, March 20). No "saintly men." *Richmond Times-Dispatch.* https://richmond.com/news/local/education/williams-the-objective-is-not-to-make-saintly-men-out-of-the-presidents-in-virginia/article_04c65f8e-48db-5017-ac7c-3c119f6a5ab9.html

Part VII

HONORING COMMUNITY CULTURAL WEALTH

This final section addresses the under-considered influence of communities in human development. Iheoma Iruka both outlines the ways communities affect developmental outcomes and shares a framework for valuing the assets that exist in every community. Jaclyn Vasquez and Mark Nagasawa describe Jaclyn's work mobilizing communities for children, while Eva Ruiz and Rafael Pérez-Segura show how early years programs can be infused with community cultural wealth and have struggled but survived even during COVID. Anna Lees concludes with a call to decolonize the field by embracing a relational ethics that is not just about human relationships but about people in relation to the land.

CHAPTER 19

Elevating the Cultural Wealth in Communities of Color

The R.I.C.H.E.R. Framework–Intersectionality Between Race and Place

Iheoma U. Iruka

Child and family development and well-being are shaped by contexts that include family, home, neighborhood, work environments and conditions, and the policies that shape them (National Academies of Science, Engineering, and Medicine [NASEM], 2019). Contexts can create multiple risks (and protective factors) that can accumulate over time and impact opportunity, experiences, functioning, and well-being. The science is clear that:

> There are specific risk and protective factors that affect health and development at multiple levels (e.g., individual, family, neighborhood, and systems/ policies). Racism and discrimination are crosscutting factors that perpetuate structural inequities and thwart healthy development for specific groups . . . Exposure to multiple risk factors . . . can lead to an accumulation of risk over the life course and ultimately result in poor health outcomes . . . Conversely, exposure to positive exposures and buffering experiences can promote health and resilience for children and adults. (NASEM, 2019, p. 143)

Thus, there is a need to recognize that context is dynamic and that a context can be promoting or inhibiting due to multiple and complex factors, including racism.

INTERSECTIONS OF RACE, PLACE, AND ECONOMICS

Land and place have been used as a form of economic, social, and psychological oppression or privilege. For example, Native Americans were forcibly removed from their ancestral lands and Black people were forced to live in "undesirable" areas of communities with limited opportunities to build wealth. There remains the continued intersectionality of race, place, and economics. Kneebone and Reeves (2016) find that Black and Hispanic people are likely to live in communities facing many social, economic, and health disadvantages compared to white people (see Table 19.1). These racial disparities and disadvantages are also seen in different geographic settings—city, suburb, small metro, non-metro. Blacks are more likely to live in disadvantage in city and non-metro communities compared to whites; Hispanics are more likely to live in disadvantage in city and suburb communities compared to whites. While data exist for certain minoritized communities (e.g., Black, Latine/Hispanic, Asian), data are limited for Native American people and their communities, resulting in even greater silence and invisibility of their issues and challenges.

The impact of race, place, and poverty has also been seen when examined through the lens of COVID-19. Figueroa et al. (2020) found that the proportion of Black and Hispanic populations across cities and towns in Massachusetts was associated with higher rates of COVID-19 during the first few months of 2020, and this also led to likelihood of death. They found that factors such as foreign-born noncitizen status, household size, and job type appear to explain the higher COVID-19 case rates among Hispanic populations, but not within Black communities. Figueroa and colleagues (2020) postulate that, potentially, for Black communities this may be due to the historical legacy and structural inequities that lead to higher incarceration rates, living in multi-unit residential buildings (e.g., projects), and neighborhood segregation that limits access to high-quality health care and exposes one to environmental toxins such as lead (Iruka, 2019).

National and local data note the disproportionate impact of COVID-19 on Native American and Tribal communities (Yellow Horse et al., 2022). For example, in Arizona, with one of the largest concentrations of single-race Native Americans in the United States, Yellow Horse and colleagues (2022) find that although Native Americans make up about 4.6% of the state's population, they comprise over 12% of the confirmed COVID-19 cases and 16% of COVID-19 related deaths. Structural determinants such as poverty, lack of health care, prevalence of certain diseases, and lack of water, housing, and healthy foods are part of the reasons for Native Americans being vulnerable to COVID-19, which are in turn linked to a historical legacy of oppression and exclusion, and lack of access to basic infrastructure and economic drivers, similar to other minoritized populations and communities.

While all Americans *felt* the pandemic in some way due to job, family, and friend loss, or even the "normalcy" of their life, this was not felt equally across people and communities. The reasons for disparities in experience

Table 19.1. Intersection Between Race, Place, and Poverty in the 100 Largest Metro Areas

	Black	Hispanic	White	All races/ethnic.
Low-income (150% below the federal poverty level	29.8%	32.0%	12.7%	19.3%
Poor locale (living in areas where more than 1 in 5 are poor)	35.6%	31.0%	9.5%	17.6%
Doubly disadvantaged	24.2%	27.6%	8.7%	14.9%

Source. Kneebone & Reeves, 2016.

are not just rooted in individual decision-making, but also due to systemic inequities that made people and communities vulnerable, such as living in households and communities with limited access to adequate food and shelter, well-staffed and resourced clinics and education settings, and jobs that provided protections.

ELEVATING COMMUNITY CULTURAL WEALTH THROUGH A CRITICAL CONSCIOUSNESS LENS

However, the essays in this book emphasize the importance of dual consciousness and being able to see beauty in the midst of tragedy and opportunities in the midst of oppressive and dehumanizing systems. These authors remind us that we must use a critical consciousness to examine how racism, classism, and other white supremacy tools operate to impact the psychological, social, health, education and economic conditions and opportunities of a community. Critical consciousness helps one examine how white supremacy is embedded (intentionally or unintentionally) in the life, law, and culture of the United States, resulting in nonwhite ways, such as Blackness, being viewed as deficit or inhuman. When a critical conscious lens is activated, Blackness, for example, is no longer viewed as the problem, but instead anti-Blackness and the harsh, oppressive, and exclusive practices, policies, and systems are (Delgado & Stefancic, 2001). Consequently, Black, Indigenous, Latinx, and other communities of color can authentically function in ways where they are not dehumanized, oppressed, or excluded from opportunities and healthy outcomes.

This is made visible by Lees in Chapter 22, who reminds us that we can agree with and support the importance of high-quality early education programming and services, but how this looks and functions must be examined through a critical consciousness to ensure that it is not eliminating Indigenous and culturally grounded processes and ancestral knowledge that elevate children's talents and gifts by harnessing the power of family, kin, land, and water. That is, to decolonize early education processes, standards, goals, and outcomes, they must be critically examined with the lens of how the settlers' colonialism is evident in the social, economic, and educational structures that may not result in the betterment of nonwhite children. Ruiz and Pérez-Segura's essay in this section reminds us that the white-dominant and white-normative processes and approaches have not resulted in better outcomes for children, families, and communities, calling for expansive ways to address major social problems and crises. Vasquez and Nagasawa's essay in this section suggests ways to identify and elevate community voices, knowledge, and resources in particular contexts for children's greater benefit. Furthermore, given that Black, Indigenous, and other communities of color continue to thrive even under a system that systematically discriminates against them and does not value their experience and expertise, there is a clear need for activating their cultural wealth.

Yosso's (2005) Community Cultural Wealth model calls on the activation of the strengths and assets of Black, Indigenous, Latine and other communities of color, which include aspirational, linguistic, familial, social, navigational, and resistant capital, especially in response to structural racism and systemic inequities. *Aspirational capital* is the ability to maintain hopes and dreams for the future, even in the face of real and perceived barriers. Even with loss of a job due to the pandemic, as was the case of so many, educators/caregivers were still inspired to use their skills and talent to provide an educational environment that mattered for their communities even if the system did not see the value and purpose. *Linguistic capital* is the intellectual and social skills attained through communication experiences in more than one language, style, or dialect. Ruiz and Pérez-Segura naming their school *Mi Casita* and leaning on Ruiz's grandmother's words *"No hay mal que por bien no venga"* (translated: *every cloud has a silver lining*) makes visible how home languages are assets that translate and transmit on multiple levels and can also inspire one to look beyond themselves and their current condition. *Familial capital* is the cultural knowledge nurtured among kin that carries a sense of community history, memory, and cultural intuition. This is described by Lees in discussing how early education needs to see and nurture children's development through *kinning*, which is a process that leverages experiences and experts from the extended family (blood and non-blood relatives) to more-than-human relations (e.g., plants, rocks, trees, animals).

Social capital is the network of people and community resources that provides instrumental and emotional support to navigate through society's institutions. This is evident in the ways diverse communities have come together to create their vision of a community that meets the needs of children, families, educators, and the whole community; this is evident in several examples Jaclyn Vasquez and Mark Nagasawa illustrate in

Chapter 20. Connecting their social capital, which included their education expertise and network, allowed them to imagine and create a new space for learning. Another cultural asset is *navigational capital*, which is the skill of maneuvering through social institutions not created with communities of color in mind. In both Lees' and Ruiz and Pérez-Segura's essays, they identify how they are seeking to maneuver through institutions while bringing to bear their cultural and indigenous thinking and processes. For example, Ruiz and Pérez-Segura continued to provide the culturally responsive learning environment desired by their children and families at Heketi Community Charter School even if it was not valued. Similarly, Lees seeks to examine how indigenous learning and processes can be integrated into traditional required and *universalized* processes and standards. *Resistant capital*, the knowledge and skills fostered through oppositional behavior that challenges inequality, is evident in visible ways such as in Ruiz and Pérez-Segura's example of how families fought to keep their school open because it was an emotionally responsive and community-focused education setting, though it was not deemed effective by the education system operators. Resistance can also be invisible, such as having the freedom to think of new ways of learning that embrace ancestral land and knowledge, indigenous ways of knowing and operating, and centering the relationship among children, families, and communities.

Scholars often highlight how *spiritual capital*, an ability to seek and lean on religious and spiritual guides, rituals, and lessons to cope with and manage life challenges, has been highlighted as a tool, process, and type of institutions that have helped Black, Indigenous, Latine, and other communities of color to thrive and cope in a racialized society that seeks to oppress and silence their spirit (Butler-Barnes et al., 2012; Spencer et al., 2003). Religious institutions have also been critical in the fight for social justice and civil and human rights (Small, 2006).

USING THE R.I.C.H.E.R. FRAMEWORK TO ELEVATE COMMUNITY ASSETS

These examples tell us that to ensure we are advancing equity in communities of color, we need to engage in R.I.C.H.E.R. actions:

Re-education is focused on learning about the true history of the United States, including the attempted eradication of the Native community and the enslavement of Africans to be the country's main economic engine. Part of changing one's mindset is to understand the history of oppressional and brutality, and classism.

Integration focuses on the authentic connection of people, communities, and especially the learning spaces. The 1954 *Brown v. Board* *of Education of Topeka* ruling showed that the idea of separate-but-equal was not equal in light of the inequitable resources and opportunities. While integration never emerged in many schools or communities, community leaders must ensure that resources and opportunities are integrated especially for underresourced communities.

Critical consciousness is an approach to understand how systemic racism and biases work. Recognizing the process of how communities are set up to benefit the few requires deep reflection, interrogation, and inquiry. Community change requires a level of self-interrogation that seeks to understand the way oppressive systems operate in order to be effectively dismantled.

Humility must be embedded in community leaders, organizations, and agencies that are gatekeepers to information, access, and opportunities. Community leaders must know and acknowledge their privilege and power and ensure that it is used to provide a liberatory space for marginalized communities and members to have agency.

Erasure of racism in all its forms is necessary for community liberation. Equity is an action, and it is critical to move beyond deficit lenses about communities of color and poor communities and using only white, middle-class standards as markers of success, ability, and excellence.

Reimagination is a lens that must be activated to create a context that provides equitable access and experiences to ensure that all children, regardless of their race, language, religion, or other social identities, know they matter. We must revise our definition of what it means to be successful. We must nurture the genius of all children in ways that capture their spirit and imagination.

REFERENCES

Butler-Barnes, S. T., Williams, T. T., & Chavous, T. M. (2012). Racial pride and religiosity among African American boys. *Journal of Youth and Adolescence*, *41*(4), 486–498.

Delgado, R., & Stefancic, J. (2001). *Critical race theory*. New York University Press.

Figueroa, J. F., Wadhera, R. K., Lee, D., Yeh, R. W., & Sommers, B. D. (2020). Community-level factors associated with racial and ethnic disparities in COVID-19 rates in Massachusetts. *Health Affairs*, *39*(11), 1984–1992.

Iruka, I. U. (2019). *Race and racism in early childhood education*. Exchange.

Kneebone, E., & Reeves, R. V. (2016). *The intersection of race, place, and multidimensional poverty*. https://www.brookings.edu/research/the-intersection-of-race-place-and-multidimensional-poverty/

National Academies of Science, Engineering, and Medicine. (2019). *Vibrant and healthy kids: Aligning science, practice, and policy to advance health equity*. National Academies Press.

Small, M. L. (2006). Neighborhood institutions as resource brokers. *Social Problems*, *53*(2), 274–292.

Spencer, M. B., Fegley, S. G., & Harpalani, V. (2003). A theoretical and empirical examination of identity as coping. *Applied Developmental Science*, *7*(3), 181–188.

Yellow Horse, A. J., Yang, T-C., & Huyser, K. R. (2022). Structural inequalities established the architecture for COVID-19 pandemic among Native Americans in Arizona. *Journal of Racial and Ethnic Health Disparities*, *9*(1), 165–175.

Yosso, T. J. (2005). Whose culture has capital? *Race Ethnicity and Education*, *8*(1), 69–91.

CHAPTER 20

It Really Does Take a Village

Why Educators Need to Be Involved in Community Initiatives

Jaclyn Vasquez and Mark K. Nagasawa

I (Jaclyn) believe the village does raise the child. As educators, we are important to children's upbringing; however, as Iheoma points out in her chapter, we're not the only factor that's necessary for children to reach their fullest potential. The community, or proverbial village, is essential for children's success and well-being.

If we recall Bronfenbrenner's (1978) and Maslow's (1943) theories, we know that children are raised with both micro and macro, up-close and far-away, influences. For children to enter classrooms ready to learn, families and children (because they do not stand alone) must have their needs met by their communities. As a young educator, I didn't understand this.

I could recite theory but didn't understand that for my students to be successful, the onus didn't rest solely on my shoulders, nor did the burden of responsibility fall completely on parents. I didn't understand that a community could come together to build robust systems of support for all families. I didn't know this because the narrative around student *success* or *failure* is always attached to a pointed finger.

Parents point to the school: "You have them for the day, so it's *your* responsibility." Teachers often point back, making assumptions (often racially and culturally biased) about families' failures to get involved in their children's learning. Federal and state policies reinforce this finger-pointing and reduce funding for schools based on failures (often identified as poor test scores and failing to make AYP—adequate yearly progress).

Low test scores are tied to racial bias, being tested in a second language, housing insecurity, being hungry and unable to focus on the test . . . David Berliner (2013) has shown that up to 60% of variance in test scores is linked to these nonschool factors—things that we had no control over. However, these factors are not a part of the narrative.

What I have come to realize is that this focus on failure—finger-pointing at the children for failing, the educators for failing, and the parents for failing—is part of our history. This is punishing children, families, and communities for *failures* that are the result of stealing lands, brutally coercing labor, and using schools to strip Native children from their families, while at the same time withholding schooling from Black children (Ladson-Billings, 2006).

I think back and realize that I was spending most of my nonteaching time helping families fill out paperwork; find food, clothing, and shelter; translating; arguing with property owners and others about basic human rights; and so forth. I actually did understand that families and students needed their needs met, but I didn't yet understand that I could be a part of *communities* coming together for children.

MY PATH TO THIS PERSPECTIVE Caminante, no hay camino, se hace camino al andar. (Traveler, there is no road. You make your own path as you walk.)

—Antonio Machado, "Caminante, no hay camino"

I do not think I ever set out to work in communities, but in retrospect, I probably always had a pathway leading here. I just had to go through my journey. My parents worked in the service of others. We always had people stopping by the house asking for *consejos* (advice) or help in general. It could be translating or taking on systems like insurance, medicine, or labor unions. Many immigrant workers were being taken advantage of, and my father would be the first one in the fight. My mother and father were always together in this.

My mom grew up in the United States as a second-generation Italian American. She knew how to navigate some systems and did most of the paperwork. If she did not know a system, she was very resourceful, and asked many questions. This was my foundation of who I am to my core.

As far as my career goes, I began as a teaching assistant. I put myself through school working 3–4 jobs, waiting tables and bartending. I worked in our family restaurant as a young kid, balancing school and community theater, and as I got older, I worked for my father in the bar and waiting tables locally, while teaching preschool and completing my associate degree, bachelor's, and then master's.

I learned about people and multitasking, grit and determination, the ability to listen, empathy, conflict resolution . . . the different experiences and opportunities afforded some but not others, the ability to meet and connect with strangers immediately upon meeting them. These are skills I used as a teacher, and that I have needed for community work: reading rooms, recalling information, and pivoting to engage and *entertain* a group of people.

When I became a teacher, I worked in 1st grade for a couple of years, and I worked in kindergarten for a minute. I taught in different spaces, from affluent suburbs, rural countryside, the inner city, to other countries. I think all these experiences working with young children and their families helped me to understand what I learned in theory, especially as I remember standing in line at WIC (officially the Special Supplemental Nutrition Program for Women, Infants, and Children), filling out papers for immigration, doing home visits, working with the community to find housing, working with a local church, looking for clothing, and helping to find food and shelter so that the kids had different things they needed in order to school ready to learn and warm and safe.

When I moved into administration in the Chicago Public Schools, as the manager of the Child Parent Centers (an early childhood and family support program that has shown long-term positive outcomes; see Niles et al., 2006), the funding was cut, and I (once again) had to be resourceful. As I started looking out into the community to see who had access to different supports and resources, I came across community collaborations. I had no idea that there were groups that were trying to support families holistically by coordinating the resources that I had spent hours, days, and weeks trying to connect with as a teacher.

I started learning about the collaborations that were working to support children and families. Many were disconnected from the school district. Everybody was working toward similar goals, yet they were not on the same page. I started partnering my schools with the collaborations that were available. I understood that they could bring resources, freeing up the funds we did have to use in another area that could equally use the funding.

What I learned through working as an administrator was that we needed families' voices, community responsibility, and policies that took into account people's lived experiences. This path brought me to the Erikson Institute (where I met Mark), which is where I spent the next 5 years collaborating with communities to create movements that brought together *grassroots* (parents, teachers, health care providers, social services, etc.) and *grass tops* (elected officials, city staff, and religious leaders), using data on children's well-being to drive action and inform policy changes.

WHAT CAN THIS LOOK LIKE?

This work took me to the "City of Prairie View" (a pseudonym) in 2018. At the time the local news was reporting that their 3rd-grade students were failing, which was devastating news for this midsized Rust Belt city that had been undergoing economic decline for decades. The school district's directors of curriculum and early childhood knew that they needed to focus well before 3rd grade, but it was just them. However, the community had two major community development initiatives—Alignment Prairie View (created to coordinate health and human services) and Transform Prairie View (which sought economic revitalization).

We started by bringing together leaders from these three groups to begin aligning goals. From there, we identified 10 different leaders who needed to champion this movement. We met with them and convinced them to get involved. From the first 10, we moved into recruiting 50 volunteers who formed the Ready to Learn movement. Through this process we discussed the current and historical issues across the community (centering children and families), thought about data that could tell stories about the community, and talked with community members (including teachers) at over 80 different functions. From that, we found the issues that floated to the top as priorities of the community: family-friendly neighborhoods and coaching for both parents and those who support them.

I kept pushing them to think about what was next, and we wrote a proposal for some initial funding, receiving a grant for $210,000 for a manager who could support the collaboration (help with planning, organizing meetings, recruiting more volunteers, etc.). We continued to add to the group, in particular in the major areas the movement identified as priorities, forming a steering committee to make plans, a community connector group (focused on linking different activities), and a policy roundtable for the mayor, superintendent, state legislators, and other local leaders to discuss policy issues and needed changes.

By the summer of 2020 we were refining the strategic action plan, had received an additional $500,000 to begin implementing parts of the plan, and had grown to 150 volunteers—in the middle of the pandemic. However, this is only the beginning. The issues that Prairie View faces (and other communities like it) aren't going to be quickly *fixed*.

WHY DO EDUCATORS NEED TO BE ACTIVE (WHEN THEY CAN BE) IN COMMUNITY INITIATIVES?

While what I am doing now, coaching community collaborations, may seem very far away from my family's restaurant or my classrooms, it's not all that different. At its most basic, what ties it all together is that I love people! I care about their experiences, and I am a person who will always work in the service of others. I get this from my parents and have used those values in all my work.

Another way that this is like teaching is that I try to build two-way trust. Whether it is with kids, parents, other teachers, or a mayor, I believe in being real and, hopefully, relatable. I am an open book, and once people get to know me, they share about their lives, too. This helps me understand what they want and need, and helps me adjust to work with them in ways that work best for them.

Just like teaching, it's hard to connect with others if they are not willing to listen to you, they do not value your opinion, or you do not value theirs. Often people think forming relationships means being nice all of the time, but it is often about being direct and having a lot of tough conversations. It takes a while until we get *there*, and lots of effort and testing (*Will she really show up like she said she would?*—I show up, driving across the state, taking that off-hours call, and otherwise jumping through the hoops), but when we get there, the conversations are amazing. Again, this is the case with children and adults.

It is also not very different from teaching in that all of it—a one-on-one meeting, a coalition meeting, a grant proposal—requires planning and reflective evaluating: What do I want to happen? What should I do? What actually happened? What data (information) am I using? What am I going to do next? How will I de-scaffold (when am I helping and when am I in their way)? Call it a lesson plan or a strategic plan. Same thing.

In the end, I'll give three answers to my question, *Why should educators get involved in community initiatives?* First, when educators play an active role in community work, they provide necessary contextual information to decision-makers and in turn become part of the decision-making process. Without families, educators, and, yes, children at the table, the lived experiences of students are not brought to light, often leading to "solutions" that do not get at the root causes of issues. Second, participating in community initiatives also sends a clear message to other community organizations that children's well-being is a shared responsibility. And finally, when a community supports the holistic needs of children, more of them can enter classrooms not only ready to learn but within schools that are ready for them.

REFERENCES

Berliner, D. (2013). Effects of inequality and poverty vs. teachers and schooling on America's youth. *Teachers College Record, 115*(12). http://www.tcrecord.org/content.asp?contentid=16889

Bronfenbrenner, U. (1978). The social role of the child in ecological perspective. *Zeitschrift für Soziologie Jg., 7*(1), 4–20.

Ladson-Billings, G. (2006). From the achievement gap to the education debt. *Educational Researcher, 35*(7), 3–12.

Maslow, A. H. (1943). A theory of human motivation. *Psychological Review, 50*(4), 370–396.

Niles, M. D., Reynolds, A. J., & Nagasawa, M. (2006). Does early childhood intervention affect the social and emotional development of participants? *Early Childhood Research & Practice, 8*(1). https://ecrp.illinois.edu/v8n1/niles.html

CHAPTER 21

Mi Casita

How a School Can Exist to Meet the Needs of Children and Adults Alike

Eva Ruiz and Rafael (Rafa) Pérez-Segura

The American education system, as it stands, often proves to be impatient, insensitive, restrictive, and punitive. In other words, it often models the least humanizing aspects of our wider society. Mi Casita Bilingual Preschool and Cultural Center in Brooklyn, NY, is built on the fundamental belief that meeting basic needs, allowing for trust to develop, and providing invitations to explore what is meaningful to children and adults alike is necessary to maintain and expand on our humanity. We believe that educational spaces such as Mi Casita are like forests, complex ecosystems of relationships that allow for living beings, and groups of living beings, to flourish in their own, distinct ways. Growing Mi Casita is our attempt to make our own paths through this larger ecosystem.

This chapter is in part the birth story of Mi Casita. Here we, Eva Ruiz, the executive director, and Rafa Pérez-Segura, the education director, share the disorientation and exhilaration of this endeavor. Through a disjointed-yet-connected narrative, readers will get a sense of how we have felt on this journey of developing the educational project that is Mi Casita. Now we would like to invite you into our journey for you to witness how it is evolving today.

A SNAPSHOT OF PRESENT-DAY MI CASITA

Three-year-old Jonathan and Frederick pick up the orange phone in the loft. Frederick thrusts his blue gloves on and brandishes a red helmet with the symbol of two hatchets crossed making an X. Maestra Teresa asks, "¿Para qué es el teléfono?" He stretches his arms out, shrugs, phone still in hand, and in English responds, "It's an emergency!"

In the excitement, Jonathan is tripping over his words: "We need to be careful because firefighters are careful." Two more "firefighters" join. One immediately muses, "We have to be careful because there is a fire." The other chimes in, "There's a baby. Let's go help them!" Waving the others over, all four firefighters and their maestra run down the stairs to save the baby.

EVA'S STORY FROM MI CASITA THROUGH THE PANDEMIC (2019-2020)

Opening a school is a Herculean undertaking in that it requires great strength of mind, body, and courage. Opening a school during a pandemic, on the other hand, is much more Promethean, like stealing fire from the gods, in that it not only requires the traits of the latter but also innovation, rebelliousness, creativity, and boldness.

After months of delays, Mi Casita finally received its New York City Department of Health license in December 2019, but only 2 months later COVID caused all early education programs to close, so 2-year-olds were forced to sit in front of a computer for remote instruction for the rest of the school year.

Now it's summer 2020 and the city tells us we can open our doors again. Twenty-four families that had committed dropped out at the last minute, leaving us with only eight students for September. The staff, disheartened by the setbacks and the quarantine, have decided not to return to Mi Casita, and all I can think about is the same thing that held me through the construction phase of this project: "I am too deep in to turn back now."

RAFA'S STORY FROM DEATH OF A CHARTER SCHOOL TO MI CASITA

Heketi Community Charter School circa November 2019:
   "How does your administration hold you accountable?"
   I respond, "Well, when something is off, they come to us to talk, and we find a solution."
   "Okay, but that's coaching and support. I asked how your administration holds you accountable."
   All three of us look at the person from the SUNY Charter Schools Institute (CSI) with confused faces. He adds, "For example, does he put anybody on improvement plans if their data is not up to snuff, you know?"
   My colleague responds, "Oh, of course not!" I think to myself, "Oof, wrong answer." I add, "Well, we don't expect to know whether or not someone is on an improvement plan; that's something between our admin and the teacher."

"Sure, but would you think it could happen then?" We all nod, "I guess so."

Despite a demonstrably strong culture and community, SUNY CSI decided to close Heketi Community Charter School. It is a death that many are still mourning.

Out of a job I loved, in the midst of the COVID-19 pandemic, I searched through endless lackluster job descriptions until I came to: "Mi Casita is looking for an Education Director with a command of curriculum design and implementation, a deep inclination towards social justice and creativity, a thorough understanding of the Reggio Emilia approach to learning, and industry experience in an early childhood educational setting."

Ever since observing the beauty of Bing Nursery School on Stanford's campus, I had wanted to learn with very young children. In retrospect, the interview between Eva and I was love at first sight. Both of us could feel a mutual admiration for humanity and teaching and a deep respect for children. I got the job.

Believing in the project that is Mi Casita, I cautiously accepted a steep pay decrease in search of a vision of early education that I am committed to, in lieu of higher-paid positions I refuse to stand by.

SNAPSHOTS OF PRESENT-DAY MI CASITA (CONTINUED)

Three *maestres* lounge back on their seats with their tea and coffees, grinning and reflecting on what one had witnessed the previous day in the classroom. The teachers and I (Rafa) watch a video of the aforementioned "emergency" from the day before. As soon as the video is finished, we describe what we see. I feel that the team is electrified with thoughts, ideas, and interpretations of what is going on.

We agree that the big idea here is that of what roles we and others play in our lives, especially around helping. We decide that the next step in furthering our students' knowledge will be transitioning from our current exploration of firefighters to what it looks like to help others.

*   *   *

The morning rays of winter sunlight pierce the storefront windows and warmly embrace the maestres in the classrooms as they are putting the finishing touches on the classroom before the kids, or, as we call them, *amigues* (friends) arrive. Lately some *amigues* have been showing interest in tape, cardboard, and Post-its. One *maestre* has set up an assortment of cardboard organized by size, with different-colored painter's tape carefully placed on the perimeter of the table, inviting anyone who comes to wonder what they can explore or do.

As we open our doors, one child, Rodolfo, rushes in as his father casually walks after him. He has already pulled up his sleeves and is dutifully washing his hands. He looks at his father and smiles with his eyes as his mouth is under his mask: "*Me estoy lavando las manos!*"

"*Hola, familia! Rodolfo, te ves súper animado! Que planeas hacer hoy?*" the teacher asks. Rodolfo looks into his classroom and observes what is set up: the cardboard and tape, the crayons and paper, the blocks and the books, the paint and the paper.

Rodolfo then jerks his eyes to the bathroom. He forgot to dry his hands! He goes to pull out the paper towel himself, throws it away in the wastebasket, and walks back. He remembers to put his things in his cubby and, with a quick *adios* to his dad, rushes toward the cardboard and tape and begins combining pieces together. Every morning our teachers, like researchers, take notes or pictures on how children engage with the environment to later reflect in our planning meetings. Besides taking notes, the other imperative of a Mi Casita teacher is engaging children through great questions.

The teacher asks Rodolfo and three other children who have joined him, "What are you collaborating on?" One child is preoccupied with how to make the structure bigger. So the teacher asks, "How might we make it bigger?"

Children begin chatting away with opinions, thoughts, and ideas. The teacher suggests making a drawing of what they want. As the children draw their ideas, the teacher writes down their ideas verbatim on large poster paper. One child, who is particularly interested in learning to write, eagerly asks to be the note-taker. Together the teachers read their ideas back to themselves.

*   *   *

Our vision for all staff is that they feel both empowered and respected enough to suggest ways Mi Casita can grow. While observing the classroom teacher, a novice teacher suggests an idea of how her role can be more impactful for the school as a whole. By supporting the classrooms in documenting what is happening, she can also create a file of videos, photos, and quotes that can more easily be shared with families. She notices that being present and documenting can be a challenge at times for teachers. Rafa suggests that she pilot her idea and, once a little fleshed out, propose it to all *maestres* for review. Once proposed, the entire team offers advice, questions, and feedback.

Through our well-defined Collaborative Advice Process, the novice teacher's idea is widely embraced and implemented. The Advice Process is used for everything from pedagogy to purchasing, and has served us well to create a spirit of true collective accountability.

*   *   *

In the 2's classroom, a teacher notices *amigo* Samuel looking in the mirror, opening and closing his mouth. At that moment, she wonders what Samuel is interested in about the mouth. In her notes, the teacher hypothesizes what the child might be doing and thinking.

To test her ideas, the teacher decides to bring out a mirror during snack and put it in front of him. Samuel takes a bite, opens his mouth, looks in the mirror, swallows, and opens his mouth again. His eyes brighten as he realizes the food is no longer there! The teacher narrates, in Spanish, "You took a bite, and then saw food. You swallowed the food, and now where did it go?" Soon enough the whole snack table is engaging in a similar exploration. The developing conversation suggests that children are interested in where things come from and where they go. Before long, the pedagogical team decides the major thread of inquiry that is emerging is related to the question of "Where do things come from? Where do things go?" From this one simple moment came an entire exploration of origins and destinations that explored not only food and our bodies but 100 different ideas.

*   *   *

MI CASITA AS A WINDOW INTO EARLY CHILDHOOD EDUCATION

As the *amigues* leave school each day, the Mi Casita team, naturally exhausted from a day spent with young children, find themselves not only ready to rest, but also to reflect, plan, and enjoy the cycle of discovery and co-creation anew each day.

Mi Casita values thinking, questioning, emotional and physical safety, socializing, creating, planning, dreaming, art, play, rest, imagination, investigation, hypothesizing, and an environment of collaboration for the entire community: children, families, and teachers. Unlike the metrics valued by many of the policymakers, Mi Casita evaluates success by the ability to hold space for the moment-to-moment and to enjoy the day-to-day, while respecting children's and teachers' individual paths.

The broader story we also want to illustrate is one that focuses on an early childhood program that was started at the beginning of COVID and has survived despite many trials. It is thriving now because we fought for it. We believe in its purpose, and its need within a system that prioritizes the bureaucracy over the ultimate purpose, and is overly standardized, demeaning, and often alienating. Mi Casita as a program respects the humanity and the strengths and wishes of its children, families, and its educators. As a living organism, it started with an idea that the community embraced and nourished. We grew something for one another.

CHAPTER 22

Sustaining Our Futures Through Expanded Relations

Anna Lees

Advancing equitable life chances across complex social contexts that are mediated by power in the form of settler colonialism and white supremacy requires educators to navigate current educational landscapes while maintaining a clear focus and commitments to bringing about the futures we desire. Such a complex balance exists in the contexts depicted through the chapters in this section and are necessary for educators working to engage a process of decolonization (Smith, 2021) while simultaneously enacting Indigenous resurgence. By this, I mean that early childhood educators committed to racial equity must both resist and disrupt settler colonialism, as it takes place in school through standardization (Lees et al., 2021), while also enacting community lifeways that have been passed down for generations (Corntassel, 2012; Simpson, 2017). While school-based standardization is manifested in early learning through mandated assessments, licensing requirements, food restrictions, age segregation, and so on, we can commit to resist such consequences of colonization by offering inquiry and land-based learning experiences. Such commitments and the necessary structures to foster inquiry and land-based learning are in need of further development and expansion, and the authors in this section have depicted important practices that engage children, families, and communities in an effort to transform early learning spaces by navigating settler colonialism in schooling and child care.

To continue efforts of decolonization, including racial equity, in early childhood education, we must consider the depth to which settler colonialism drives social structures such as capitalist economies and the subsequent impact on education (Wolfe, 2006; Yellow Bird, 1999). With this, we must recognize the ways in which social structures, including systems of education, are designed and take place within our natural world. Considering deeply how complex ecosystems and relationality must frame equity efforts is emerging in the design of Mi Casita (Ruiz & Pérez-Segura, Chapter 21) and in educators' involvement in community initiatives (Vasquez & Nagasawa, Chapter 20). Such endeavors set the foundation for further decolonization and Indigenous resurgence through applications of land education for young children, families, and communities that disrupt core constructs of schooling shaped by the violence of colonization (Bang, 2020; Nxumalo, 2019). Furthermore, understanding Indigenous approaches to teaching and learning as extended networks of relationality, or kinship, offers a framework to meaningfully engage decolonization, along with humanization, as valued at Mi Casita, in early learning toward just and sustainable futures. I am cautious in making recommendations around kinship in educational settings that were designed to sever familial networks. To be clear, Indigenous education premised on kinship is complex and occurs within deeply grounded social and community values and ways of being, and should not be perceived through a romanticized or utopian lens or as a checklist of ideas that can be easily espoused.

INDIGENOUS RELATIONS

Indigenous peoples across global geographic regions have engaged complex processes of teaching and learning within intergenerational contexts between humans and more-than-humans since time immemorial (Cajete, 2015; Deloria & Wildcat, 2001; Simpson, 2014). In these contexts, children are nurtured to develop their individual gifts and to understand their roles and responsibilities within and across communities. Learning from human and more-than-human relations offers a system of education premised on kinship, and in this, children have opportunities to observe, listen, practice, and develop in flexible and responsive contexts. Education premised on kinship offers an environment where children are nurtured by relatives and have opportunities to learn from caring peers, older youth, adults, and elders, as well as lands, waters, and other more-than-human relations such as plants, rocks, trees, and animals. Much like the example depicted at Mi Casita, considering early learning through a lens of relationality sets forth opportunities for all children and families to once again have positive learning experiences in formal settings. In an education system guided by relationality, as Indigenous education has always been, teaching and learning do not take place with rigid expectations and timelines for development or closed-ended expectations of outcomes, or apart from lands, waters, and community. Similar to the Prairie View example, Indigenous education is not a practice that takes form away from the rest of community. These systems of education exist today within Indigenous communities outside school settings and are returning in early learning programs where educators are creating spaces "built on the fundamental belief that meeting basic needs, allowing for trust to develop, and providing invitations to explore what is meaningful to children and adults alike is necessary to maintain and expand on our humanity" (Ruiz & Pérez-Segura, Chapter 21). However, the onset of colonization, and with it racism and capitalism, have made these educator commitments and community ways of knowing and being incredibly difficult to maintain in school-based settings.

The inception of capitalism as the assumed economic structure within the United States radically shifted the ways in which education takes place (Tuck, 2013) and the design and accountability of early childhood education (Lees et al., 2021). One aspect of this is the drastic shift in education away from a network of kinship to the separation of children from their families for most of their waking hours, often beginning in infancy, with exceptions for some family child care and kith and kin networks of care (Ashley J. May in Chapter 4). Forced separation from family, however, took place historically through boarding schools and has continued with compulsory schooling and expansion of public early learning, in large part to foster capitalist labor structures (Tesar, 2015). While I am very much in favor of high-quality early learning, we must not forget that the good intentions of such spaces have historically been to eradicate Indigenous peoples (in an effort to gain ownership of land) by removing children from their families, languages, and cultures in the most impactful time of development. This occurs through a model of distancing children from their communities to secure a labor force and impacts a wide range of children and families outside the privilege of white affluence or other social positionings deemed worthy of sovereign futures. Such practices of education for harm and assimilation have been forced upon Black, Indigenous, and Communities of Color and are often promoted as good-faith support by nation-state governments in the form of public or public/private funding for birth-to-age-5 education. To take seriously commitments of decolonization, such nation-state efforts must be perceived with caution in how such funding can serve as the continuation of colonization.

Engaging networks of kinship as a framework for early learning offers an opportunity to reimagine the structure of schooling back to a family and community endeavor. Van Horn et al. (2021) theorize kin as a verb, *kinning*, where

> being kin is not so much a given as it is an intentional process. Kinning does not depend upon genetic codes. Rather it is cultivated by humans, as one expression of life among many, many, many others, and it revolves around an ethical question: how to rightly relate? (p. 3)

If we consider kinning as an underlying premise of early learning, we have the opportunity, and I suggest responsibility, to frame curriculum design with the overarching question of *How do we rightly relate?* Such a question serves as an opening to live in good relations with expansive networks of kinship, including more-than-humans, where all peoples may thrive. What if we engaged all children in ethics of relationality rather than discrete skill-based instruction and did so within intergenerational contexts? What if teacher and educational leadership roles prioritized and were rewarded for "coaching community initiatives" (Vasquez & Nagasawa, Chapter 20)? I imagine a structure where families can connect within neighborhood or geographic regions, in both urban and rural settings, to foster learning with and from lands and waters. Where teachers and educational leaders work to facilitate such experiences and serve as resources for family and community-based schooling, instead of serving as the sole adult educator (or one of few) with an increasingly large group of young children.

My assessment of the goals of publicly funding early learning is not to contradict the importance of early childhood education or to say that robust education systems should not be widely accessible, but to question how those goals can be achieved within a capitalist state that requires the elimination of Indigenous peoples and lands and the exploitation of Black and Brown laborers to secure settler futures (Tuck & Gaztambide-Fernández, 2013). Simply put, can a settler state have a role in decolonizing education while actively maintaining capitalism? While I do not have expertise to make recommendations around global economic reform to engage sustainable futures, I will speak to ways I believe early learning can be visioned beyond a social service used to secure a labor force toward corporate gains.

Opening the boundaries of school-based education is a grand effort of social transformation. Chapter authors in this section have articulated their commitments to continue dreaming forward while making change in the current moment. Such dreaming is in good company with efforts across the field of redeveloping curriculum with a focus on living in right relations. Anishinaabe scholar Megan Bang has done extensive work on this topic (Bang, 2020), and with colleagues developed both Indigenous community-based (see Indigenous STEAM: http://indigenoussteam.org) and school-based (see Learning in Places: http://learninginplaces.org) resources for engaging teaching and learning in relationship with lands and waters across generations. These resources offer opportunities to support teacher preparation and professional development to expand land and water education and consider the roles of teachers in collaboration with families, communities, and Indigenous nations. These efforts, like the chapter contributions in this section, offer a concrete beginning to reshaping school-based learning toward inquiry experiences that positively shape children's relationships with human and more-than-human kin. I encourage others to access this important work and continue developing their commitments to developing land and water education across early learning settings.

CONCLUSION

Highlighting examples of early learning opportunities toward decolonization offers hope toward more expansive change. While I do not expect these shifts to occur across public education immediately, the radical adaptation of school-based education at the beginning of the COVID-19 pandemic offers insight on how quickly change can happen (e.g., reunification of children and families, elimination of testing requirements, rapid food security initiatives). I believe we can develop much more permeable boundaries between school and family/community and eliminate the practice of a single lead teacher as the primary facilitator of teaching and learning. It is possible for parents and caregivers to continue working and also engage in their children's education if a network of kinship or relationality is enacted and if employers imagine organizational models with basic flexibility. Eliminating age segregation (e.g., grade levels or age-based classrooms) as a premise for organizing early learning settings and desired outcomes would also support the reinstatement of kinship in education toward goals of living in right relations. I am deeply interested in understanding processes of decolonization in our current moments. Taking active efforts to engage education grounded in kinship with lands, waters, and one another offers opportunities to secure thriving futures and life chances for all of our relations.

REFERENCES

Bang, M. (2020). Learning on the move toward just. *Cognition and Instruction, 38*(3), 434–444.

Cajete, G. (2015). *Indigenous community.* Living Justice Press.

Corntassel, J. (2012). Re-envisioning resurgence. *Decolonization: Indigeneity, Education & Society, 1*(1), 86–101.

Deloria Jr., V., & Wildcat, D. (2001). *Power and place.* Fulcrum Publishing.

Lees, A., Vélez, V. N., & Laman, T. T. (2021). Recognition and resistance of settler colonialism in early childhood education. *International Journal of Qualitative Studies in Education.* http://doi.org/10.1080/09518398.2021.1891319

Nxumalo, F. (2019). *Decolonizing place in early childhood education.* Routledge.

Simpson, L. B. (2014). Land as pedagogy. *Decolonization: Indigeneity, Education & Society, 3*(3), 1–25.

Simpson, L. B. (2017). *As we have always done: Indigenous freedom through radical resistance.* University of Minnesota Press.

Smith, L. T. (2021). *Decolonizing methodologies.* Zed Books.

Tesar, M. E. (2015). Te Whāriki in Aotearoa New Zealand. In V. Pacini-Ketachabaw & A. Taylor (Eds.), *Unsettling the colonial places and spaces of early childhood education* (pp. 108–123). Routledge.

Tuck, E. (2013). Neoliberalism as nihilism? *Journal for Critical Education Policy Studies, 11*(2), 324–347.

Tuck, E., & Gaztambide-Fernández, R. A. (2013). Curriculum, replacement, and settler futurity. *Journal of Curriculum Theorizing*, 29(1), 72–89.

Van Horn, G., Kimmerer, R., & Hausdoerffer, J. (2021). *Kinship, volume 5*. Center for Humans and Nature Press.

Wolfe, P. (2006). Settler colonialism and the elimination of the native. *Journal of Genocide Research*, 8(4), 387–409.

Yellow Bird, M. (1999). What we want to be called. *American Indian Quarterly*, 23(2), 1–21.

Now What?

Our Call to Collective Action

Mark K. Nagasawa, Lacey Peters, Marianne N. Bloch,
and Beth Blue Swadener

What is transformative change? What does it mean to transform early years policy? And what is my place in that? These are big questions. The number, scope, and scale of our colleagues' recommendations may seem daunting. However, none of this is as difficult or problematic as leaving things the same, simply surviving within a narrow vision that reinforces what is, rather than what could—and should—be. Participating in transformative change means leaving comfort zones, joining and extending the conversations included in this collection, challenging the status quo by asking hard questions, sitting with discomfort, and embracing collective action and activism as a part of our professional toolboxes.

While this collection takes on the breadth and complexity of early years (care and education) policies, programming, and practices, it is unified by recognizing two things. First, that the United States's fragmented systems are pervaded by racism, sexism, classism, ableism, adultism, and related oppressions; and second, that many folx are beginning to join together for collective national and local change. Our call to action is to join this resistance through the kind of convivial research and creativity contained in this book (Callahan, 2018). Some of our colleagues' recommendations involve shifts in thinking (e.g., recognizing inequities within the early years field, enacting culturally grounded, caring-centered program policies, curricula, and budgeting decisions), while others involve changes to federal, state, local, and community administrative structures and practices. Transformation's linchpin is identifying how small, local actions can be a part of bigger changes.

INTEGRATING THE SMALL AND BIG

Twenty years ago Lourdes Diaz Soto and Beth Blue Swadener (2002) argued for a radical rethinking of early years policy, practice, and research, with the recommendation to start with "our own modest lived experiences" (p. 52). It was sound advice then and remains so. Quite often we read authoritative publications where the authors speak as if they have always been experts. Here we asked many of our colleagues to write personally, to give us glimpses of their personal or professional challenges and how these relate to transformative ideas and actions. By humanizing these issues, our aim has been to show that possibilities exist, even with difficulties and within complexity.

Their stories illustrate ways to locate ourselves within these issues and systems. Drawing on our experiences and pooling our energies, we can challenge racist, classist, paternalistic, and adultist perspectives about the early years' value. They help us better understand why the term "just babysitters" is particularly demeaning to the infant-toddler workforce (Part III). Our colleagues' powerful writing about the sharp divisions between who is a child care provider and who is an early childhood educator—what they look like, the languages they speak, the ages of the children in their care, and where they do their care work—also illustrates the reality that words and beliefs do more than emotional harm; they result in material harms like differential pay, benefits (another form of pay), and working conditions (Parts II, III, IV, and V). Our beliefs matter.

When we speak about notions of quality or professionalization, our colleagues remind us to always ask, *Whose ideas or beliefs about quality and professionalism are being centered? Who and what are we omitting from the conversation?* Once we identify a belief system that is a barrier, we can examine and change it. Transformative change in early years policies requires this because these rules telling people what to do are expressions of beliefs and values.

Our colleagues in this collection call us to envision a society that values and includes diverse knowledge systems in its programs (e.g., labor force, children, curriculum, assessments, and regulations). They also ask us to challenge perspectives and practices that focus on assimilating and standardizing children, families, and educators to white, middle-class, gendered, and able-bodied norms (Parts IV, V, and VI). But how will we get there? To reiterate, we think that large-scale transformations begin with ourselves.

As our colleagues in this book assert, transformative change lies at the confluence of the personal, interpersonal, institutional, and structural (introduced in Part II), with relationships, caring for each other, or *"kinning,"* as Anna Lees calls it, at its core (Part VII). On the surface, this advice may not seem all that transformative, but, as many of our colleagues have shown, engaging in this kind of reflection—collectively—will lead to a critical mass movement challenging dominant beliefs, curriculum, professional teacher education guidelines, quality rating systems, and more. Rather than tinker at the edges with tiny changes, we hope this volume urges deeper and broader changes in beliefs and action.

This brings us back to the question we posed at the outset: "How do we condition the possibility of something else?" The following section explores what is possible, providing a synopsis of our recommendations followed by examples of advocacy tools that can help you contribute to transforming early years policy in the United States.

TRANSFORMING BELIEFS

Recommendation 1

Focus on an equitable start in life for all children as a shared, public responsibility.

Again, transforming social beliefs that shape policies begins with each of us. Questions to ponder include: Do I really believe in a shared responsibility for young children? What are the ways my beliefs contradict this? For example, what are ways that we have internalized the idea that child care is *not educational*, is *not real school*, is *just babysitting*, and that, ultimately, it is a *private/family responsibility*? (Lucinda Heimer in Chapter 1; Chrishana Lloyd and Julianna Carlson in Chapter 6; and Emmanuelle N. Fincham in Chapter 8). What are my underlying assumptions about race, languages, disabilities, poverty, age, queerness, and particular neighborhoods, and how do these play out in my context? A shared public responsibility for equitable early years for all children means confronting how each of us is implicated in *othering* different groups of children, families, communities, and colleagues when we interpret, implement, and make policies (including ones in our classrooms and other early years settings). This kind of courageous honesty is important, but it cannot end there.

Recommendation 2

Actively challenge and transcend deficit assumptions grounded in racism, sexism, classism, adultism, and other forms of oppression.

When a critical conscious lens is activated, Blackness, for example, is no longer viewed as the problem, but instead anti-Blackness and damaging practices, policies, and systems are understood as the real problem. As Iheoma Iruka argues (along with Ashley J. May, Chrishana Lloyd, Julianna Carlson, Kerry-Ann Escayg, and Flóra Faragó in Part II and Evandra Catherine in Part VI), transformation will happen when "Black, Indigenous, Latinx/e, and other communities of color can authentically function in ways where they are not dehumanized, oppressed, or excluded from opportunities and healthy outcomes" (Iruka, Chapter 19, p. 145). Our active opposition to systemic oppression is a prerequisite for change at every level.

Recommendation 3

View all children, families, and educators as competent and rich in knowledge.

The conversation in Part VI, "Whose Standards?," emphasizes that respect for the cultural and linguistic assets children and families bring with them is crucial for revamping the one-size-fits-all approaches to curriculum, teaching, and learning that accrediting bodies, teacher preparation programs, and Quality Rating and Improvement Systems (QRIS) promote as best practice (also in Parts IV, V, and VII). Subtly embedded in these white, middle-class dominant approaches are normative and exclusionary assumptions that inevitably lead to either/or judgments: meeting/not meeting a standard. A key takeaway from Part VI is the necessity of engaging in *both/and* thinking as a way of discovering new pathways between our equity-aspirations and assimilationist, standards-based practices.

TRANSFORMING PROCESSES

Recommendation 4

Listen to children and meaningfully engage them in decision-making around matters that impact their daily lives.

This recommendation addresses a notable absence in our collection. Ageism, in the form of adultism, is deeply embedded in the early years field, with a long history of thinking that children are in need of extra care, adult protection, and education because they are incompetent. These adultist beliefs have led to a rights-curtailing underestimation of young children's interests, knowledges, and experiences. Adults who care for and educate young children and/or who make decisions about their life experiences must be attuned to their views and perspectives, and gain deeper understandings of how adultist orientations toward them limit their human potential by overprivileging a narrow set of academic outcomes (what Louis Hamlyn-Harris called "relentlessly teleological" in Chapter 2). This necessitates challenging unreflected-upon beliefs about children as vulnerable, in need of protection, and *at risk for failure* should they lose access to *high-quality* programming.

It also means calling out *whole-child* approaches to early years research, policy, and practice that do not recognize children as protagonists, social agents, collaborators, and contributing members of society. As protagonists, young children must be acknowledged as being multifaceted, experienced, capable, competent, and active participants in their lives. As citizens, children's views need to be taken seriously, given *due weight* in shared decision-making, and a part of conversations about their school and life experiences. This shift toward anti-adultism must also include *ensuring* that programs and schools are *ready for children* (Jaclyn Vasquez and Mark Nagasawa, Chapter 20), instead of pressuring them to be ready for later schooling (Iorio & Parnell, 2015).

Recommendation 5

*As a public good, **everyone** should be at the table.*

Lea Austin (Chapter 10) asks how compensation policies could be developed and prioritized among broader early care and education initiatives if members of the workforce were actively involved in constructing policy. Betzaida Vera-Heredia notes the injustice of "policies *done to people, not with people*" (Chapter 12), and Jaclyn Vasquez and Mark Nagasawa (Chapter 20) illustrate ways in which alliances between local governments and an array of community organizations have led to grounded policy-making, community-based needs assessments, integration of resources, and more humanizing approaches to strategic planning. It is crucial that early years policies reflect the voices of those impacted and most heavily concerned.

Throughout this volume, we have read calls for implementing and transforming legislation, policies, systems, and funding through collective action. This recommendation calls for alliances among diverse community experts, including children, families, caregivers/early educators, health care providers, representatives of business, and local, state, and federal government officials, to advocate for change. These alliances should have appreciation for local strengths and preferences but be charged with developing guidelines and guideposts for local communities (e.g., infant health guidelines), as well as guidelines for states to develop equitable systems of provision and funding for early years care/education from birth to 5 years.

TRANSFORMING THE WORKFORCE'S VALUE

Recommendation 6

Question and reconceptualize the notion of who qualifies as a professional and what qualities and credentials count.

In the call to establish a unifying framework for the early childhood profession, NAEYC's Power to the Profession (P2P) initiative (http://powertotheprofession.org) defines who is *in* very narrowly and in ways that privilege teacher education and credentialing. Whiteness, class, and age intersect, enabling some to more smoothly access higher education and certification. This has resulted in a devaluing of many with years of experience and vast knowledge of culture, language, and community, as emphasized by Jacqueline Jones in Chapter 3; Ashley J. May in Chapter 4; Juliana Pinto McKeen, Fabiola Santos-Gaerlan, Alice Tse Chiu, Wendy Jo Cole (representing the Brooklyn Coalition of Early Childhood Programs, Chapter 11); and Betzaida Vera-Heredia in Chapter 12; and Lorraine Falchi and Cristina Medellin-Paz, in Chapter 15. A competency- or equivalency-based system should be used to allow those with excellent and long-term experience to remain as teachers/caregivers in the field.

In addition, members of the Brooklyn Coalition of Early Childhood Programs remind readers that "caregiving is a human trait" and that the people who work in early care and education settings must embody the relational, social, and emotional qualities needed to nurture children's well-being and teachers' ability to thrive (Eva Ruiz and Rafa Pérez-Segura, Chapter 21). Caring relationships with children, families, their communities, and each other are core professional competencies.

Recommendation 7

Move from "essential but expendable" to "essential and valuable."

Recommendation 1 calls for a shift in the belief that young children's care and education is a private responsibility to recognition that it is a societal responsibility. The research evidence is clear that the early childhood period (prenatal through age 8) is very important in children's development and learning. In addition, the increase in the number of working parents has shown that good child care is crucial for families and for a strong U.S. economy. Therefore, the entire early years workforce, including those who work in home-based, public, and private settings, must be acknowledged as "essential and valuable" and cared for accordingly by being paid living wages and benefits like health care, paid sick leave, and retirement savings (Chrishana Lloyd and Julianna Carlson, Chapter 6; Lea Austin, Chapter 10; and Abbi Kruse, Chapter 14). This leads directly to our next recommendation.

Recommendation 8

Create the public funding that is essential for compensation parity among early years professionals.

As many of our colleagues have illustrated, beliefs that child care is a private issue, not a public good, have resulted in an early years system that relies heavily on families' ability to pay for services, despite the existence of universal prekindergarten (UPK), child care subsidies, and Head Start.

Wages and benefits should recognize all caregivers and early childhood educators adequately and in an equitable way, regardless of their title or type of program. As Lea Austin (Chapter 10) argues, "No one working to care for and educate children should be worried about how to feed their own families. They should be able to perform this essential service without trading off their own well-being."

The simple fact is that compensation for the early years workforce cannot be raised, nor what families pay for private care lowered, without a major increase in public funding (Emily Sharrock and Annie Schaeffing, Chapter 9). While President Biden's Build Back Better plan, which included substantial funding for universal preschool and increased child care subsidies, has not yet passed into law, the importance of public funding for early care and education is now part of public dialogue. We can play a part in moving these proposals from discussion into policy by participating in multilevel collective action (local, state, and national).

TRANSFORMING SYSTEMS

Recommendation 9

Establish new governance systems at federal, state, and local levels that integrate early years (birth–5) program provision and funding streams as a comprehensive, equitable, and coordinated system.

In Chapter 3, Jacqueline Jones suggests the bold act of consolidating all major federal early care and education programs in one agency. This agency would partner with its local and state counterparts to help programs leverage different funding (as Lucinda Heimer urges in Chapter 1 and Louis Hamlyn-Harris illustrates in Chapter 2). This new agency would be charged with developing a system of equity-centered disability services and programming for young children, including infants/toddlers, that recognizes the full range of early years settings within communities: schools, child care centers, homes, houses of worship, community organizations, and so forth; values children's rights; and honors community cultural and linguistic wealth (Yosso, 2005). It would also have to make connections with the social safety net, health care, workforce development, housing, and community development programs that can help children and their families to thrive (see Part VII).

We are under no illusions—this would be a major and messy undertaking, but there is precedent. The U.S. Department of Health and Human Services was only created in 1953 and the U.S. Department of Education in 1979. In a more recent example of administrative restructuring, in 2019 most funding for public early childhood school-based and community-based programs in New York City (i.e., child care, Head Start, and public preschool) were consolidated in the city's Department of Education. While the long-term effects of this move are uncertain, some see it as an opportunity to advance equity goals (Potter, 2019). Furthermore, states across the country are exploring how to blend and braid separate early years funding streams to support efforts like those described by Louis Hamlyn-Harris in Chapter 2. The good news is that tools exist to help administrators and program leaders to do the same; for instance, the Ounce of Prevention developed the *Blending and Braiding Early Childhood Program Funding Streams Toolkit,* a practical guide that lays out how this can be done, including providing resources and examples of how different states have gone about this (Wallen & Hubbard, 2013). While written for state administrators, those working directly in early years programs can use the policy ideas in this toolkit to shape grassroots advocacy for systems that will support and sustain their local equity work.

Recommendation 10

Establish systems and policies that are humanizing: affirming of racial, cultural, linguistic, gender, social class, and disability identities for both children and adults.

As Lucinda Heimer argued in Chapter 1, the current system is functioning according to design. Therefore, no amount of systems reorganizing will be truly transformative unless all of these recommendations are part of the new system's *blueprints.* To help show what we mean by this, we offer a historical example.

Head Start was created as a part of the War on Poverty, which was a response to the Civil Rights Movement's calls to action. What was then called Project Head Start was part of the Economic Opportunity Act of 1964, which funded social programs that still exist (e.g., Job Corps, Volunteers in Service to America, and community action agencies). A central idea in the law was "maximum feasible participation." This meant people in local communities being meaningfully involved in decisions affecting them. While, sadly, this might seem overly idealistic now, maximum feasible participation is alive today in Head Start Parent Policy Councils. These required groups are run by parents and community members who are involved in budgeting, hiring teachers, and other critical programmatic decisions (Greenberg, 1990), but this spirit is not limited to the past.

Other nations are showing that humanizing systems are possible by reshaping policies and curriculum that recognize Indigenous knowledge and cultural wealth, including culturally grounded assessment (e.g., *Te Whāriki* in New Zealand). As Iheoma Iruka, Anna Lees, and others in this volume suggest, this is happening in the United States as well. Margarita Ruiz Guerrero and Carolyn Brennan (Chapter 17) remind us that people form new relationships when they engage in critical reflection that centers *Others*. When we do this we ". . . more authentically enter into partnerships, as we can more clearly see how a history of oppression may impact the ways in which individuals interact with others" (p. 131).

Unleash the power of the profession. Several chapters suggest the potential of authentic partnerships that could be mobilized for transformational movements (i.e., the Brooklyn Coalition of Early Childhood Programs, Chapter 11; Abbi Kruse's Essential Not Expendable Facebook group, Chapter 14; and Jaclyn Vasquez's work in "Prairie View," Chapter 20). While formed during COVID-19, groups like these are potential mechanisms for advancing transformative proposals. We suspect that there are many similar groups across the United States. What if they were connected with one another? Imagine the possibilities. For example, in support of increased federal early care and education funding, NAEYC (2022) recently organized over 10,000 practitioners who lobbied Congress through emails, social media, and meetings with congressional staffers where they shared stories of families' search for high-quality, affordable early years programs and how these programs can transform lives. While increased funding has not yet occurred, organizations like NAEYC, Child Care Aware of America, and the Children's Defense Fund need grassroots support from us.

Change may be slow, but it can happen. In 2019 the state of California passed a law (AB-413) requiring removal of *at risk* terminology from schools, community resources, and professional systems serving children and youth. With this legislation, the term *at promise* replaced the term *at risk*. This law was based in part on Beth Blue Swadener and Sally Lubeck's 1995 call to avoid "at risk," which reflects racist, classist, and ableist assumptions, with a strength-orientation based upon an "at promise" perspective. This is a lived value of embracing *all* children's promise. It is a mistake to dismiss this change as mere semantics. We reassert that the beliefs we hold and the words we use inform the actions we take and how folx are impacted by them. The idea changed minds and guided the considerable advocacy needed to propose and pass this legislative revision. The next steps are putting the value of *at promise into practice*.

EXPANDING OUR TOOLBOXES: POLICY AND ADVOCACY

We are confident that when our colleagues' recommendations are put into place the United States early years systems will be transformed, but who will make these changes? Our answer is *us*, which raises the stickier question, *how*? Not to oversimplify too much, but what we propose is a basic toolbox that can be used for planning, doing, and evaluating—all of which are guided by equity-focused reflective practice.

Planning for Action

As Jaclyn Vasquez and Mark Nagasawa said in Chapter 20, planning is crucial, whether it is for a lesson or advocacy. We think this planning begins with Lourdes Diaz Soto and Beth Blue Swadener's (2002) suggestion to reflect on our lived experiences. In fact, the majority of our recommendations involve investigating our beliefs and how these appear interpersonally, organizationally, and structurally (in the policies, the rules, we follow in our professional and personal lives). It should never be forgotten that Paulo Freire (1970) argued that *reflection is action*, but how can reflection be transformed into additional actions?

Reflection is the foundation for developing what some activists call a "story of self." This is a technique for humanizing a social issue, developing your credibility to speak on it, clarifying your *why*, and setting the stage for what you want someone to do about your issue (see http://narrativearts .org; VanDeCarr, 2015). Think of the many stories of self in this collection, such as Louis's efforts to desegregate his center (Chapter 2). Ashley's reflections on being nurtured within Black kith and kin homeplace (Chapter 4). A governor telling Abbi that he knew they would stay open during the pandemic "for the children" and how she channeled her outrage (Chapter 14). Eva and Rafa making the Mi Casita dream a reality (Chapter 21). Stories are both powerful ways of connecting to others and analytic processes.

What is your story?

- Begin by brainstorming adjectives that describe you and how you want to be in the world (e.g., compassionate, smart, dedicated, stubborn . . .).
- Then brainstorm issues you care most about, ones that affect folx you know, such as those our colleagues have shared with us—pay disparities, navigating higher education spaces, and so forth.
- Now the key part: How do you connect this to your issues? What is the compelling story? What specific memories come up? Who else was a part of this? What was the setting? Use some of the essays in this book as models.

Authoring stories involves taking a lot of information and organizing it so that it makes sense to someone else. While crafting a story of self may be new and unfamiliar, you already possess many tools to help you do this, such as the ability to research, organize, synthesize, and share information.

The work of clarifying your story of self, your *why*, leads to the *what* (should be done). As a part of this process, think about some of the issues you identified.

- What do I know about the policies and systems that relate to my issue?
- What is the history of how this issue has been addressed?
- Whose vision is currently dominant?
- What are new and interesting ideas for addressing this issue? (You do not have to come up with solutions all on your own.)
- What are my assumptions about change, who should be involved, and where should it happen (e.g., federal-local/organizational, public-private, transformational-incremental, visionary-pragmatic, etc.)?

Pursuing answers to these and similar questions are essential next steps in making your advocacy path: *se hace camino al andar* (Jaclyn Vasquez and Mark Nagasawa, Chapter 20). Again, our contributors offer both models for this process and resources for further learning (i.e., their reference lists).

This leads to the next tool, crafting a "laser talk," which is the same as an elevator speech or pitch. What is key to know is that they are personal, succinctly describe problems and solutions, and involve asking your audience to do something (Swadener, 2003). However, most of us are not such gifted speakers that we can speak off the cuff about complex things. Effective laser talks require preparation, which you have already begun with your story.

To help you develop your laser talk, we suggest a framework developed by the anti-poverty organization RESULTS because it is simple to remember, freely available on the Internet, and very useful for organizing one's thinking. They call the framework EPIC, which stands for *Engage* [your audience], [state the] *Problem, Identify* [your solution], and *Call to Action* (Results.org, 2022). While all aspects of the framework are crucial, in our experience it is very common for advocates to forget about the call to action—what do you want someone to do with what you have shared, and how will you hold them accountable?

For example, imagine you are a family child care professional and want to do something about wage equity in early years programs. This is something you have experienced directly, but you have not spent much time considering how the system works. So you do some research that helps you understand policies that affect you. Now apply the EPIC framework.

You might *engage* your audience by painting a picture of the care-teaching you provide for the, mostly, infants and toddlers in your care: you look like them, you speak the languages they are familiar with, and your curriculum is activities of daily life: going to the park to explore, shared meal times, and so on. You give examples of the children you have seen grow up, the developmental milestones you observe, and why parents trust you with their children at this developmentally sensitive time in their lives. Then you lay out the *problem*.

The children's parents can neither afford to pay for the full cost of care, nor does the child care subsidy from the state Office of Child Care help cover your costs (via the federal Child Care and Development Block Grant; see Part I) because the reimbursement rate is based upon 10-year-old data. The solution you have *identified* is to use the Office of Child Care's current statewide child care market rate survey to determine reimbursements, which would be a 33% increase (fictitious), enabling you to give your assistant a raise and purchase updated materials for the children. Now the important part: your *call to action*.

Who is your audience, and what do you want them to do about changing the way reimbursements are calculated? It is very common to focus so much on what we want to say that we neglect to consider our audience(s). What is their perspective, understanding, and interest in our issue?

Your audience might be other family child care professionals and your call to action is for a group of you to show up at an Office of Child Care public meeting. The accountability piece is, who showed up? At the meeting, your call to action to those officials would be to make the updates or to get them to say why they have not made the update in 10 years. Accountability in this instance might be getting them to say what they intend to do and when or for them to publicly accept responsibility for their decisions. Your accountability in this might be to let them know that you will follow up with them in a month—and then do it.

Or your audience might be the state senator who chairs the Human Services Committee and who has made public statements that child care is a family responsibility. He is on record saying, "I spell early childhood education, M-O-M." This is where ideas drawn from cross-cultural and diversity, equity, and inclusion work can be helpful. For instance, Isaura Barrera and Lucinda Kramer (2012) developed an approach that they call Skilled Dialogue. We think that, although developed to help early childhood educators work cross-culturally with children's families, approaches like Skilled Dialogue (or any other methods of trying to bridge differences between people) is useful in advocacy, for if we all agreed on the problems and their solutions, this book would not be necessary.

In essence, Skilled Dialogue involves two main dispositions: choosing relationships over winning and "setting the stage for miracles"—being open to unthought-of solutions. Furthermore, these interactions are infused with a commitment to respect, reciprocity, and responsiveness. We acknowledge the difficulty maintaining these stances with someone who strongly disagrees with you, like the state legislator in this example. The key is to use this kind of guidance to humanize your opponent, even if they are dehumanizing you, but how?

They suggest five strategies to use: (a) staying truly open to communication, (b) allowing space for the other person to express their views, (c) trying to make sense of their viewpoint by perspective-taking, (d) appreciating the legitimacy of others' beliefs, and (e) finding common ground. As our colleagues in this collection have shown, the racist, sexist, and classist attitudes affecting the early years need to be understood as a part of our national cultural fabric. From this perspective, the state senator's beliefs become a little more understandable.

To be crystal clear, engaging in this perspective-taking does not mean agreeing with someone or excusing their attitudes' impacts (in this example, sexism, classism, and, likely, racism or xenophobia). Part of your decision-making must also include when the harm to you outweighs any potential benefits of your advocacy. Your well-being matters because advocacy is a *marathon and not a sprint*.

An additional consideration about audiences and what you are trying to persuade them to do is an idea borrowed from architect Buckminster Fuller (1963), who invented "trimtabs." These are smaller rudders that turn the large rudder(s) on a ship, with the ship being a metaphor for the ship of state. Continuing our example, this state senator is not likely to share your commitment to respect, reciprocity, and responsiveness. The process of perspective-taking—developing some understanding about his interests, positions, voting record, and so on—may lead to identifying who his trimtabs are. Who may have influence with him? This could be members of his church, a business group, another legislator, or someone like his administrative assistant. The key is to think in terms of leverage.

Doing

While all this preparatory work is *doing*, these are actions in service of engaging others in the kinds of reflection and equity-focused discussion represented by this book. Laser talks are best seen as the foundation for many different actions, ranging from delivering your talk to someone face-to-face (including to a principal, program director, or school board) to writing letters to the editor, crafting blog posts, issuing policy memos meant for more technical audiences, making public statements at protests, spreading the word through social media, and so on.

An important message to remind ourselves is that each of us cannot do this work alone. Higher-leverage collective action is how policies at *different levels* are changed (Swadener, 2003). As we have through this book's dialogic processes, we grow as advocates through the back-and-forth with others. This is how arguments and skills get refined. Collective action has the additional benefit of providing collegial support to one another to help us weather difficult interactions and tough times.

But the reality is that the labor involved in collaboration—communicating, coordinating, and cooperating—is really hard, even among those who care about one another, have similar points of view, and share goals. This is another place where approaches to conflict negotiation, like Skilled Dialogue, come into play. Sustaining collective, healing-centered action requires committing to communication, especially when it is difficult; tending spaces where multiple viewpoints are welcome; perspective-taking; appreciating the legitimacy of others' perspectives; and seeking common ground over winning.

Evaluating

Regardless of the format your advocacy takes, a critically important consideration to your call to action is building in accountability and evaluation. While evaluation is often thought of as judging if something worked or not (either/or), we think it is better thought of as taking a learning stance that focuses on reflective questions like these:

- When we were planning, we thought X would happen. What actually happened?
- Did we do what we said we would?
- What went well, and what did not?
- Did the person do what we asked of them? If not, why not?
- Did our action help anyone, even potentially?
- What information are we using to make these judgments?
- What did we learn, and how does this change our plans?
- Who are we leaving out? Who else needs to be involved?
- What will we do next?

While the toolbox we have presented is small, we think these are essential tools that will grow with you over time and with repeated practice.

FINAL THOUGHTS

We started this book with the hope of presenting ideas to the then-incoming President Biden. Later, as the book was in process, we had high expectations for the proposed Build Back Better agenda, which prioritized funding parental leave, subsidies for child care, and UPK programs for 3- and 4-year-olds (Koch, 2021). While that agenda stalled in winter 2022 amidst rising inflation, the president's plan was revived in negotiations over what became the Inflation Reduction Act. Passed in July 2022, the final version, among other things, expanded Medicare; put funding into "clean energy jobs," and addressed high energy costs (The White House, 2022). However, the new law left out inflation-combatting policies like paid family leave, child care, and expanded child tax credits (Hickey, 2022).

While it would be understandable to view these serious omissions as a failure, it is important to recognize two things. First, meaningful policy changes have happened, even if they are imperfect or partial victories. Head Start, early intervention, universal prekindergarten, and child care subsidies exist. Second, these policies did not just magically appear. People made them happen—through considerable struggle. Despite what feel like intractable political conditions, we and our colleagues in this collection are optimistic about future possibilities due to growing recognition of the early years' vital importance and the creative, equity-centered work that is being done *right now* to transform early years policy in the United States. We invite you to join this collective action.

REFERENCES

Barrera, I., & Kramer, L. (2012). *Using skilled dialogue to transform challenging interactions.* National Association for the Education of Young Children.

California Assembly Bill 413, Education: Title 1 § 96 (2019).

Callahan, M. (2018). *Convivial research.* http://ccra.mitotedigital.org/convivialres

Diaz Soto, L., & Swadener, B. B. (2002). Toward liberatory early childhood theory, research and praxis. *Contemporary Issues in Early Childhood, 3*(1), 38–66.

Freire, P. (1970). *Pedagogy of the oppressed.* Continuum International Publishing Group.

Fuller, R. B. (1963). *New forms vs. reforms. World design science decade documents.* World Resources Inventory.

Greenberg, P. (1990). *The devil has slippery shoes: A biased biography of the Child Development Group of Mississippi.* Macmillan.

Hickey, C. (2022, August 12). Not the year for women and parents: Child care provisions were cut from the Inflation Reduction Act. It's not the first time. CNN. https://www.cnn.com/2022/08/12/politics/inflation-reduction-children-families/index.html

Iorio, J. M., & Parnell, W. (Eds.). (2015). *Rethinking readiness in early childhood education.* Palgrave MacMillan.

Koch, C. (2021, November 1). *Breaking down the* Build Back Better Act. https://info.childcareaware.org/blog/breaking-down-the-build-back-better-act

National Association for the Education of Young Children. (2022). CEO Michelle Kang's statement on the Senate's passage of the Inflation Reduction Act [press release]. https://www.naeyc.org/about-us/news/press-releases/senate-passes-inflation-reduction-act

Potter, H. (2019, October 28). *Creating integrated early childhood education in New York City.* The Century Foundation.

Results. (2022, April 7). *U.S. poverty laser talks.* https://results.org/resources/2022-u-s-poverty-laser-talks/

Swadener, B. B. (2003). "This is what democracy looks like!" *Journal of Early Childhood Teacher Education, 24*(3), 135–141.

Swadener, B. B., & Lubeck, S. (Eds.) (1995). *Children and families "at promise": Deconstructing the discourse of risk.* SUNY Press.

The White House. (2022, August 19). *Fact sheet: The Inflation Reduction Act supports workers and families.* https://www.whitehouse.gov/briefing-room/

statements-releases/2022/08/19/fact-sheet-the-inflation-reduction-act-supports-workers-and-families/#:~:text=The%20Inflation%20Reduction%20Act%20lowers,union%20jobs%20across%20the%20country

VanDeCarr, P. (2015). *Storytelling and social change* (2nd ed.). Working Narratives (now Narrative Arts). https://narrativearts.org/wp-content/uploads/2016/02/story-guide-second-edition.pdf

Wallen, M., & Hubbard, A. (2013). *Blending and braiding early childhood program funding streams toolkit. Enhancing financing for high-quality early learning programs.* Start Early. https://www.startearly.org/app/uploads/pdf/NPT-Blended-Funding-Toolkit.pdf

Yosso, T. J. (2005). Whose culture has capital? *Race Ethnicity and Education, 8*(1), 69–91.

Index

About the Editors

Mark Nagasawa directs Bank Street College of Education's Straus Center for Young Children and Families, which researches the question, *What is the progressive ECE of the 21st century?* This work is grounded in being the child of an early educator-mom who started out as a classroom volunteer, became an assistant teacher, and eventually a lead teacher in Head Start.

Lacey Peters is a tenured Assistant Professor of Early Childhood Education at Hunter College of the City University of New York. Her career in early childhood education started in a preschool classroom, and she has been a teacher educator for the past 10 years. Her research explores early childhood educators' lived experiences in classrooms and examines their roles as policy enactors.

Marianne (Mimi) Bloch is Professor Emerita in the Departments of Curriculum and Instruction and Gender and Women's Studies at the University of Wisconsin-Madison. Her research has focused on historical and international comparative social policy, with specific attention to child care policy. Her publications include *Governing Children, Families, and Education: Restructuring the Welfare State* (2003) and *Reconceptualizing Early Education and Care* (2018).

Beth Blue Swadener is Professor Emerita in the School of Social Transformation at Arizona State University. Her research spans critical childhood studies, internationally comparative social policy with a focus on sub-Saharan Africa, and disability studies. A major theme of her scholarship and activism, drawn from disability justice work, is "nothing about us without us."

About the Contributors

Lea J. E. Austin is the Executive Director of the Center for the Study of Child Care Employment at the University of California, Berkeley. She leads the Center's agenda of realizing a public early care and education system that secures racial, gender, and economic justice for the women whose labor is the linchpin of its services. She is an expert on the U.S. ECE system and its workforce, and has extensive expertise in the areas of compensation, preparation, working conditions, and racial equity.

Carolyn Brennan is an Assistant Professor of Early Childhood Education at Western Washington University. She began her career as a toddler teacher and now teaches courses focused on infants and toddlers, families, behavior guidance, and equity. Her research focuses on early childhood teacher preparation and supporting teachers to advance social justice in the classroom.

Julianna Carlson is a Research Scientist at Child Trends with over a decade of experience in the early care and education field, first as an early educator and now as a mixed-methods researcher. Her research is centered on the early care and education workforce, evaluating policy and program initiatives to support ECE professionals across the country with a focus on addressing structural inequities.

Evandra Catherine is an Assistant Professor in the Mary Lou Fulton Teachers College and the Director of Leadership Development and Senior Scientist of Mental Health Equity for the Children's Equity Project at Arizona State University. Dr. Catherine's work focuses on addressing equity in policy, practices, and systems for young learners and advancing equity in early care and education through Early Childhood Mental Health Consultation.

Alice Tse Chiu is an occupational therapist, working primarily in pediatrics for almost 25 years. After struggling to find an intimate quality preschool for her two children, she decided to open one herself, one where the children feel like they are entering their auntie's home to play, rather than attending "school." She believes a child's first introduction to school should be in a very relaxed, welcoming, and comfortable environment, where the child feels very safe to simply play, explore, and create. Alice lives in Brooklyn, NY, with her husband and now grown adult children.

Wendy Jo Cole is a leader, teacher, counselor, consultant, and interspiritual Minister and Director. She is committed to the right to play and to sacred activism through the Brooklyn Coalition and Little Chairs Big Differences. She has a master's degree in early childhood educational leadership from Bank Street, a master's degree in social work from the University of Minnesota, and a bachelor's degree from Mount Holyoke College. She studies family therapy at Ackerman Institute and supervises at One Spirit Interfaith Seminary. She currently works as a matriarch and teacher at Mi Casita and spent 20 years directing Maple Street School. She is also joining The Collaborative practice as a therapist.

Stephanie M. Curenton is a developmental and community psychologist who studies the healthy growth and development of racially or linguistically marginalized children, such as Black/African Americans and dual language learners. Dr. Curenton's areas of expertise include the development of classroom quality measures as well as professional learning for teachers related to how to create early childhood classroom environments that embrace equity and diversity, and provide high-quality language learning environments.

Kerry-Ann Escayg is an Associate Professor of Early Childhood Education at the University of Nebraska Omaha. Dr. Escayg's main research and teaching interests are anti-racism in early childhood education, Black children's racial identity development, qualitative research with young children, and racial socialization. In addition to her anti-racist research and scholarship, Dr. Escayg is a creative writer and often utilizes short stories and poetry to illuminate the lived realities of racism, challenge dominant ways of knowing and being, and center marginalized and racialized voices.

Lorraine Falchi is an Early Childhood Coach at the New York Early Childhood Professional Development Institute, City University of New York (CUNY). She holds a doctorate in education from Teachers College, Columbia University. She is an inclusive, bilingual educator and teaches courses in language and literacy. Dr. Falchi is a contributor to journals including *Early Childhood Education Journal, Journal of Early Childhood Literacy,* and edited volumes such as *Multimodal Literacies in Young Emergent Bilinguals* and *Rethinking Readiness in Early Childhood Education.*

Flóra Faragó is an Associate Professor in Human Development and Family Studies at Stephen F. Austin State University. Dr. Faragó's teaching and research interests center around children's racial and gender prejudice and stereotype development, anti-bias and anti-racist teaching and parenting, and inclusive early childhood education surrounding race and gender. She collaborates with colleagues and organizations nationally and internationally, including the Indigo Cultural Center, Local to Global Justice, the Jirani Project, and the Girl Child Network. You can learn more about Dr. Faragó's work at www.florafarago.com.

Alexandra Figueras-Daniel began her career as a preschool teacher in a dual immersion school in New Jersey's Abbott pre-K program. Alex applied what she learned as a teacher to conducting research at the National Institute for Early Education Research and completed her PhD in education policy while there. Alex is a co-author of the *Classroom Assessment of Supports for Emergent Bilingual Acquisition* (CASEBA) to measure the quality of language supports for dual-language learners (DLLs) in preschool classrooms, and co-developed the system using the related *Self-Evaluation for Supports of Emergent Bilingual Acquisition* (SESEBA) for use by teachers and coaches. In 2021 Alex was awarded a Young Scholars Program grant from the Foundation for Child Development in 2021 to investigate coaching and professional development of Latina preschool teachers working with DLLs.

Emmanuelle N. Fincham, Assistant Professor of Early Childhood Education at Western Washington University, has spent the vast majority of her teaching career as an infant/toddler teacher at the Rita Gold Center at Teachers College, Columbia University. She holds a doctorate in curriculum and teaching and is actively engaged in early childhood research and teacher education. The bulk of her research focuses on toddlers and those who teach them, aiming to reconceptualize understandings of practice, play, and young children's development and ways of knowing.

Lucinda Heimer, Professor of Early Childhood Education at the University of Wisconsin-Whitewater, has published articles, chapters, and a book on early childhood policy using critical theory and ethnography to illuminate perspectives of identity, race, and social justice centering equity. Dr. Heimer has taught university courses on curriculum, racism, and ECE policy; supervised students; taught in preschool and elementary classrooms; and worked as a center director. Her work spans public, private, and tribal settings.

Louis Hamlyn-Harris is an Executive Manager at Early Childhood Australia (ECA), focused on supporting child and educator mental health. He has worked as an early childhood teacher and leader in a variety of settings in Australia, Vietnam, and the United States. Prior to joining ECA, Louis served as Senior Director of Early Childhood at a major nonprofit in New York City. He lives in Melbourne, Australia.

Iheoma U. Iruka is a Research Professor in Public Policy and Founding Director of the Equity Research Action Coalition at the Frank Porter Graham Child Development Institute at the University of North Carolina at Chapel Hill. Dr. Iruka is focused on ensuring that racially minoritized children, especially Black children, are thriving through the intersection of anti-racist and culturally grounded research, program, and policy. Dr. Iruka serves on numerous national and local boards, including the National Advisory Committee for the U.S. Census Bureau and the National Academies of Science, Engineering, and Medicine.

Jacqueline Jones is President and CEO of the Foundation for Child Development. She was Deputy Assistant Secretary for Early Learning in the U.S. Education Department and Assistant Commissioner for Early Childhood Education in the New Jersey State Department of Education. Dr. Jones was a Senior Research Scientist at the Educational Testing Service in Princeton, NJ. She attended Hunter College and earned a master's and PhD from Northwestern.

Abbi Kruse is the founder and Executive Director of The Playing Field, an early childhood program serving children experiencing homelessness right alongside those from far more advantaged families. Prior to this role, Abbi served in a variety of ECE settings, including the University of Wisconsin Preschool Lab, Head Start, and community-based programs. She is the organizer and principal administrator of a Facebook group titled Essential Not Expendable that has over 8,000 members.

Anna Lees (Waganakasing Odawa, descendant) began her career as an early childhood classroom teacher in rural northern Michigan. Now an Associate Professor of Early Childhood Education at Western Washington University, Dr. Lees works to develop and sustain reciprocal relationships with Indigenous communities to engage community leaders as co-teacher educators, opening spaces for Indigenous values and ways of knowing and being in early childhood settings and higher education. Her research forwards land and water education for curriculum and professional development with tribal nations and early learning programs.

Chrishana M. Lloyd, Senior Research Scientist at Child Trends, is a nationally recognized expert on the study and implementation of interventions to support early care and education professionals. She has more than 20 years of experience in research, evaluation, technical assistance, and dissemination of research findings to inform policy and practice. In most of her work she uses a racial equity lens and partners with community members, practitioners, and other key stakeholders to inform the projects she undertakes.

Ashley J. May is an ethnographer of childhoods and the Founder and Project Director of the Grassroots Morning Garden Project. Through community-engaged, Black feminist ethnography and oral history, she explores the everyday, place-attuned liberatory practices among Black and Brown caregiver/child dyads. Ashley's current project, a three-volume research zine titled *Thirty Sunsets and a Moon*, is held at the UMass Amherst Black Feminist Archive and the Barnard College Special Collections Zine Library.

Cristina Medellin-Paz is an Early Childhood Career Coordinator at the New York Early Childhood Professional Development Institute, City University of New York (CUNY). She holds a doctorate in developmental psychology from the CUNY Graduate Center. Her research examines the systems and structures that support the workforce through professional development and stackable credentials for the Latinx/e family child care community. She applies a critical lens in her research that uplifts and affirms communities of color.

Barbara Milner is passionate about children and supporting the adults who care for them. Over 30 years in this field, her roles have included teacher, family child care provider, director, and project manager. A consultant since 2002, she's worked with professional development programs and coordinated coaching for quality improvement projects. Her experience includes national and international work, including traveling to over 20 Air Force bases in five nations and across the United States, providing professional development support. Recently, she worked with NAEYC, supporting the development of National Early Learning Standards for Infants and Toddlers, and facilitated leadership training in Saudi Arabia. Currently, Barbara works with Central Arizona College on early childhood initiatives.

Rafael (Rafa) Pérez-Segura is the son of Mexican immigrants. Rural eastern Connecticut and Mexico City feel like home. Within the last decade, Rafa has taught several in dual-language contexts. He is now the Education Director at Mi Casita. He is passionate about providing children and families with the highest quality of care, love, and pedagogy. He has a master's in elementary education with an authorization in bilingual education from Stanford University's Graduate School of Education.

Juliana Pinto McKeen is a social worker, licensed therapist, and activist in Brooklyn, New York. Juliana was the director of Honeybirds Playschool, an accredited Waldorf program. Honeybirds was open for 7 years before closing due to the COVID-19 pandemic. Juliana holds a BA from Hunter College in psychology and a master's degree from Columbia University in social work. Additional publications include "Mind the Gap: Addressing

Childcare Inequalities for Children and Caregivers" in the *Columbia Social Work Review.*

Vanessa Rodriguez is an Assistant Professor in the Center for Early Childhood Health and Development at the NYU Grossman School of Medicine. A veteran K–12 educator, Dr. Rodriguez conducts qualitative and mixed-methods research that amplifies educators' perspectives using humanizing, trauma-informed, and social justice-oriented methods. Her work has been funded by the National Science Foundation, the Foundation for Child Development, the Early Childhood Research Network, and the Spencer Foundation, among others. Her current funded projects employ critical feminist frameworks to better understand and advocate for educator mental health and wellness, particularly among Black and Latina women in early childhood education.

Eva Ruiz is the Founder and Director of Mi Casita and a lifelong educator. She has worked as a teacher, researcher, and policy advisor. Eva has been a teacher in the United States and internationally. She has also conducted research at NYU's Metropolitan Center for Research on Equity and the Transformation of Schools. Eva served as Education Policy Analyst and Budget Manager for New York City Council member Letitia James, and later worked as a Political and Community Affairs Director at the New York City Department of Education. She received her bachelor's degree in psychology from the University of San Francisco and her master's degree in the sociology of education from the Steinhardt School at New York University. Eva currently serves on the board of Parents Together.

Margarita Ruiz Guerrero is an Assistant Professor of Early Childhood Education and is part of the Education for Social Justice minor at Western Washington University. Her research has explored Latinx children's disconnections between home and Head Start food experiences near the Mexico/U.S. border. Currently, her work is related to the experiences of students registered in an early childhood teacher preparation program aligned with and equity-social justice curriculum.

Fabiola Santos-Gaerlan is the Founder and Executive Director of Honeydew Drop Childcare, an early childhood program with five locations serving the Brooklyn community since 1999. After a career as a television producer for 15 years, Fabiola changed course. She came to the realization that she was happiest when working with children while she was on assignment interviewing children of all ages across the country. Fabiola then dedicated herself to opening Honeydew Drop. She holds a B.A. in communications and a master's in TV production, and has a credential in program administration. She is also a state-certified Parent Educator.

Annie Schaeffing is Director of Strategic Initiatives at the Bank Street Education Center. She provides strategic advisement and research support for external partnerships and manages communications for the Learning Starts At Birth initiative. Annie previously focused on early childhood workforce development at the Office of the State Superintendent of Education in Washington, DC and began her career as a Head Start teacher in Phoenix, Arizona. Annie holds a master's degree in education policy from American University.

Emily Sharrock is Associate Vice President of the Bank Street Education Center. She has spent over 20 years working in education policy, leadership, and administration. As a Network Leader in the New York City Department of Education, Emily oversaw the leadership, instructional, and operational support provided to more than 25 schools spanning K–12. Emily has also worked as an instructional and leadership coach in early childhood and K–12 settings. Emily holds an MPA from Columbia University's School of International & Public Affairs.

Mariana Souto-Manning, PhD, is Erikson Institute's fifth president. She has served as professor of education at Teachers College, Columbia University and held additional academic appointments at the University of Iceland and King's College London. Mariana is committed to the pursuit of justice in early childhood teaching and teacher education, and her research centers the lives, values, and experiences of intersectionally minoritized people of color. Mariana has coauthored more than 10 books, dozens of book chapters, and over 85 peer-reviewed articles. She has received several research awards, including the American Educational Research Association Division K Innovations in Research on Diversity in Teacher Education Award.

Jaclyn Vasquez is an educational consultant with expertise in special and multilingual education, parent empowerment, curriculum design and development, play and adventure-based learning, pre-K-to-kindergarten transitions, data for racial equity, strategic planning, grant writing, and professional development. She holds a B.S. in early childhood special education, an M.S. in early childhood and bilingual literacy, and is a doctoral candidate in curriculum design and leadership. She was co-director of the Policy and Leadership Department at the Erikson Institute, manager of the Chicago Public Schools' Child Parent Centers, and an early childhood classroom teacher for many years.

For more than 20 years, **Dr. Betzaida Vera-Heredia** has worked in a variety of capacities to support young children, families, and early childhood professionals. Her most significant contribution to the field is acting as a Cultural Broker to ensure that ECE workforce members' voices are heard and valued, especially those from underrepresented and underserved communities. Her role as a broker relies on her expertise in issues related to culture, gender, and race. She has facilitated professional learning opportunities at both national and international levels. She has been successful in developing and improving policies that enhance the quality of learning and professional development opportunities available to educators and trainers. She is passionate about implementing innovative ideas and strategies to better support the workforce in accessing high-quality learning and professional development resources and tools for empowerment. She is committed to educators and trainers and helps them to navigate the system in culturally relevant and meaningful ways.